THEMES AND ISSUES IN MODERN
SOCIOLOGY

The Sociology of Fertility

GEOFFREY HAWTHORN
*Lecturer in Sociology, University of Essex,
England*

COLLIER-MACMILLAN LIMITED LONDON
The Macmillan Company

Collier-Macmillan Limited
10 South Audley Street, London W1

The Macmillan Company,
Collier-Macmillan Canada Ltd, Toronto

Copyright — Collier-Macmillan Limited, 1970
Library of Congress Catalogue Card Number: 69-10538

First printing 1970

Printed in the Republic of Ireland
by Hely Thom Limited
Dublin

CONTENTS

iii

PREFACE

In this brief review, I have chosen to interpret 'the sociology of fertility' as the study of the social determinants of human fertility, and reluctantly decided to forego the opportunity to discuss some of the consequences of particular fertility patterns. To have attempted both would have stretched my competence and meant sacrificing what I considered to be essential details of fact and interpretation. Ronald Freedman, in his 1961-62 *Current Sociology*, has already summarised much of the work on the social determinants of fertility, and it is only necessary to supplement him because of the large amount of good research (for much of which he himself is responsible) that has been published in the interval. I have concentrated disproportionately on the later work, and my review should not be taken to replace his. It is merely a second attempt to perform that task, necessary to what Thomas Kuhn has called 'normal science', of trying to codify the work of others. Much remains to be done, and the measure of my book's success will be its irrelevance in a few years' time.

The book really has a second author in Joan Busfield, who has worked with me in this field for the past three years, and whose hard work, high standards and constant enthusiasm have contributed to what coherence my argument possesses. I have no doubt that its shortcomings coincide exactly with those points at which I stubbornly resisted her detailed comments. I am also grateful for the patient and constructive criticism of the editors, to the University of Essex for granting me leave in which to finish writing, and to Marion Haberhauer for unscrambling my dreadful draft into a typescript.

Suffolk: August, 1969

CHAPTER I

Introduction

Populations are the product of birth, migration and death rates. Demography is the name conventionally given to the study of the nature and interactions of these rates in human populations, and of the effects of changes in them on the composition and growth of such populations. Since its units of study are rates, it is an aggregative science, and since these rates can be given a precise numerical weight, also a quantitative one. It is also an area of inquiry in which, by comparison with almost all other social sciences, the supply of data is very good indeed. For obvious practical reasons most states have long kept more or less precise records of the composition of the populations under their jurisdiction, and these records, supplemented in recent years by the results of studies commissioned for more scholarly purposes (purposes which coincide with general social utility and which therefore receive relatively adequate financial support), provide an enormous fund of information upon which to draw. This is not to say, of course, that this information is all of the most useful kind. The development of the cohort approach in demographic studies of fertility, for example, which I discuss in the next chapter, has made demands on the data that cannot be met from many censuses. And some of the most interesting historical questions, for example about the exact demography of the population increase in Britain in the eighteenth century, relate to periods that antedate censuses.

In order to delimit a practicable field of study, all sciences select a more or less narrow range of phenomena from the infinite connected web and tend to treat the relationships within this field as a closed system. Demography is no exception. Its system consists of the three rates mentioned above, together with closely associated factors like the age structure. Moreover, given the numerical character of their data, demographers tend to express the systemic inter-relationships in a formal way. The classic example is Lotka's (1925) model of a 'stable' population. A population is said to be stable if it has a fixed age and sex distribution, if the mortality and fertility rates[1] at each age are constant, and if there is no outward or inward migration. From these postulates, it follows that the weighted average mortality and fertility rates over any range of ages must be constant, and thus that the overall birth and death rate must also each be constant. The difference between them, which is the net annual rate of change in the numbers, is also constant. In consequence, the population develops in geometrical progression, except in the special case in which birth and death rates are exactly equal, and where, therefore, the population is stationary. Stability, so defined, can only be achieved if the same age-specific rates of mortality and fertility have been in force for something like a century. No large population has ever achieved such stability, and it is not likely that one ever will.

The postulates of the stable population theory are rarely met, but the difficulties that this poses are not my problem here. My point now is to use the example of the concept of the stable population to illustrate the nature of demographic models. The demographer's question is either 'given the rate x and the set of population parameters y, what follows for the composition and growth of the population?' or 'given what we know about the population already, what can we say about rate x, which we do not know?' Other scientists interested in population variables do not make the analytical assumption that populations are closed systems. Their questions would be 'what non-demographic factor or factors give rise to rate x, and what are the consequences of rate x in turn for these factors?' These two sorts of questions are not, of course, alternatives. They are complementary. The demographer is interested in the relationships within the system. The others are interested in how the elements in the system interact with their environment. Sociologists are curious about the connections between strictly demographic variables and other social factors.

Practically and theoretically, the most important element in the system of population variables is now fertility. World popu-

[1]Various measures of fertility are discussed in Chapter II.

lation is growing at about 2 per cent per year, a rate that implies a doubling in size every thirty-five years. Now that death control on the scale that has long been familiar in the more advanced industrial societies has spread to most developing areas, and that international migration is accounting for less and less of the variation in any population, fertility rates have become crucial. Coale (1965) has illustrated this with a dramatic calculation. In a fictitious population with the very high gross reproduction rate (the ratio of replacement for each married woman on the assumption that she survives through to the end of the reproductive period) of 4·17 recorded for the Cocos-Keeling Islands and the high expectation of life of seventy-five years recorded for Sweden, the annual rate of growth would be 5 per cent. Were all members of this imaginary society to suddenly achieve immortality, it would only increase to 5·1.

Almost all classical theories of the causes of fertility rates have assumed that fecundity[2] is constant. Bizarre hypotheses, such as that which suggested a causal connection between the spread of bicycle riding among married women and the decline in the birth rate a century ago, have been the exception rather than the rule, at least in recent years. Those theories which can be taken seriously fall into two groups (U.N., 1953; Eversley, 1959). The first, and more famous, is the Malthusian. The second is usually described as 'the standard of living theory.'

Malthus (1798; 1803 *seqq.*) starts from three premises: first, that sexual passion is constant; second, that 'population . . . increases in geometrical progression of such a nature as to double itself every twenty-five years'; and third, that 'the means of subsistence . . . could not possibly be made to increase faster than in an arithmetical ratio'. His deduction, with a minor premise, is that 'by the law of nature which makes food necessary for the life of man, the effects of these two unequal

[2]English-speaking demographers use 'fecundity' to mean reproductive potential and 'fertility' to mean reproductive performance. This is the reverse of the biological and French demographic usage. French demographers have adopted the concept of 'fécondabilité' to describe the probability of conceiving in a given period (usually a menstrual cycle). This has passed in direct translation into English demographic usage. I adopt the usage of English-speaking demographers here.

powers must be kept equal. This implies a strong and constantly operating check on population from the difficulty of subsistence.' Reading Malthus carelessly, it would seem that he considers starvation to be the only check to population growth. This is a misleading inference. Malthus distinguished between what he called positive and preventive checks. The first are all causes of mortality, and the second voluntary limitations of births. By referring to the first group as vice and misery, and to the second as moral restraint and vice, Malthus confused the issue with High Anglican ethics, but the point is clear. The three possible checks are voluntary birth control, mortality by means other than starvation and—lastly and ultimately— mortality from starvation. It is a logically complete model. All that remains is for weights to be ascribed to each of the three assumptions, none of which can safely be assumed to be constant, and to each of the variables.

In the course of the revisions and elaborations that Malthus made of his original essay, he concentrated less on the possibility of populations controlling their numbers with positive checks and more on the reality that he began to notice in early industrial England of couples controlling their fertility to maintain or improve upon their standard of living. Empirically, it became clear that preventive checks were intervening long before the ultimate tragedy of death by starvation. Towards the end of his life, he predicted that the price of food would fall relative to other commodities, that the lower classes would restrict their families to keep to the same nutritional level, and that, moreover, they would acquire a taste for other commodities that would further serve to restrict their fertility. The point was put clearly by Alfred Marshall in the 1880s: 'the average age at marriage depends chiefly on the ease with which young people can establish themselves, and support a family according to the standard of comfort that prevails among their friends and acquaintances; and therefore it is different in different stations in life.'

It was a short logical step from this argument, but a long empirical one, to the proposition that each population is in an optimal relationship with its environment, with the supply of critical resources. Marshall's hypothesis becomes an axiom: it is assumed that the population is allocating its resources optimally. Having made this assumption, theorists using the notion of an optimum population ask how a balance is achieved between population density and the available resources. They ask what it is that holds back the latent power of increase so that resources are not over-exploited (Carr–Saunders, 1922; Wynne–Edwards, 1962). Not only is the assumption almost certainly too strong, but the question is very difficult to answer. Carr–Saunders and Wynne–Edwards tend to talk of an optimum population size in some static sense, and this, of course, becomes unrealistic in advanced societies in which the resource-base is continually changing. In such societies, it is more sensible (although analytically still extremely difficult, especially when one considers the fact that both values and facts enter into the calculations) to talk of optimum rates of population *growth* (Ohlin, 1967).

It is not surprising that no one now accepts the Malthusian contention that people will breed at a constant rate until the resources are extinguished, since Malthus himself abandoned it except as a theoretically possible limiting case. The alternative contention, that people will breed at a rate consistent with maintaining or even improving their standard of living, fits more easily with the facts. It does so, however, at a price. If the standard of living is interpreted in a narrow sense, then the contention cannot account for those couples who decide to have a certain number of children to satisfy an emotional need or a religious prescription. If, on the other hand, the standard of living is interpreted in a broad sense, equivalent say to 'quality of life', the contention becomes effectively vacuous. It begs the questions of what standards among what groups in what societies at what points in time. The particular meaning of 'standard of living' in any situation demands empirical illustration. To a very large extent it demands sociological illustration, since sociologists are those in the academic division of labour who are charged with relating norms to behaviour, and to a lesser extent with accounting for the norms themselves, whether historically or in terms of some reductive factor. It may be that there are different hierarchies of different norms in different societies, and that no cross-cultural generalisations are possible. Or it may be that there is more similarity in the nature and arrangement of norms and their interpretation across cultures than might at first appear. It is an empirical question. The hope is that one will eventually be able to produce valid generalisations that steer the precarious course between triviality and vacuity, and it is to this hope that the remainder of the book is addressed.

CHAPTER II

Definitions and Measures of Fertility

1 FERTILITY RATES

As I implied in the discussion of the Malthusian and standard of living theories at the end of the previous chapter, most sociological studies of fertility take it as the dependent variable and assume that various social factors are the independent ones. To begin with, I shall therefore discuss the various ways in which fertility can be measured.

For most purposes, the simple sum of births in any registration area, unrelated to any other figure, is not useful. The simplest useful measure is the crude birth rate, which is the number of births per thousand population per annum. If one is concerned with the balance of numbers in the whole population, this may be all one needs. For example, a crude birth rate that exceeded the sum of the emigration and death rates would imply population growth, and *vice versa*. Most refined measures of fertility adopt the same principle of relating the number of births to a base defined in space and time, and achieve their refinement simply by refining this base. The general fertility rate takes the married women in the child-bearing years as its base; the age-specific rate takes the married women in specified age-groups as its base. Both bases are usually standardised to the statistic of 1,000 women per annum in the relevant category. The total fertility rate is the sum of age-specific birth rates and thus, although calculated on the same base as the general fertility rate, is more precise than the latter, since it takes into account variations in the distribution by age of fecund women. The gross reproduction rate is the number of daughters that would be born per woman in a group

7

of women, all surviving to the end of the reproductive period and bearing daughters at each age in accordance with the rates prevailing among women of various ages in the area and during the period under consideration. It is in fact essentially the same as the total fertility rate, except that it takes female births only. The net reproduction rate takes into account the woman's likelihood of living through the fecund period and weights the estimate accordingly. It is, therefore, always slightly lower than the gross reproduction rate, since in no population do all women survive through to the end of the fecund period at menopause. The ways in which these rates are constructed are discussed in detail in most demographic texts (Barclay, 1958; Cox, 1966; U.N., 1965). The ways in which they reflect what is going on in a country over any period can be seen from the United Nations' *Demographic Yearbook* volumes devoted to natality, or births, the most recent of which relates to 1965. Part III, the Commentary, of the Registrar General's *Statistical Review* of England and Wales, which is usually published three years after the year in question, does this for these two countries.

Taken as I have described them, these rates all refer to one period in time, usually a year. Demographers refer to them as 'period' rates. However, most of the really pressing questions about fertility, including those of a kind that might interest the sociologist, are about the trend of fertility over time. Consider a table of age-specific birth rates, with the years for columns and the ages for rows. Two sorts of time series can be derived from this table. One would be a sum of the columns, so that by reading along the bottom of the table one could trace the trend of the total fertility rate from year to year. The other would be a calculation of the total fertility rates for women born in a particular year by tracing a particular group or cohort of women diagonally across the table until they disappear at the end of the fecund period. The first time series is a period one; the second a cohort one. The former is concerned with what is happening to all women at one point in time; the latter is concerned with what is happening to one group of women over time. The adoption of cohort analysis is probably the most important analytical advance in post-war demography. Its adoption comes not from any intellectual insight, but from the relatively recent availability of data that enable it to be calculated. The ages at which women bear their children, for example, were not recorded in this country until 1938, nearly ninety years after the need for such information was expressed. The logic and usefulness of cohort analysis have been examined by Ryder in a series of excellent papers (1956; 1959; 1964a; 1964b).

The general usefulness is easily apparent. A cohort analysis shows that the rising birth rates in Britain and the United States in the years after the Second World War were due to a very large extent to a postponement of births coinciding with young married couples having children earlier and at shorter intervals than their parents, a pattern that has been emerging more and more clearly since the general fertility decline set in towards the end of the nineteenth century. The classic cohort studies are those made by Glass and Grebenik (1954) for the Royal Commission on Population and by Whelpton (1954) in the United States. All the more recent field studies of fertility and some of its social correlates, the studies that I discuss later in the book, have taken the cohort as their starting point. For reasons determined largely by the ways in which the respective censuses tabulate their data, Americans tend to use 'cohort' to mean a group of women born in the same period, and the British to mean a group of women married in the same period.

These are not, however, the only possibilities. Ryder has concisely summarised the process of childbearing as a series of dated steps (1965), and from this summary it is clear that a cohort could rest on a number of bases. There are six variables in the set that describes the dated steps: population membership and age; marital status and marital duration; birth parity and birth interval. These are arranged in pairs, each pair consisting of a status acquired by the occurrence of an event, and the length of time since that occurrence. (Parity is the number of children born; and the birth interval is the interval between marriage and the first birth, or between one birth and the next). Two American field studies have taken as their units of analysis samples of women from the cohort who have already had two children (a parity of two) with the purpose of finding out if they expect to have any more and, if so, why. A further refinement (adopted in both these studies) is to break down these parity-specific rates by age. An age-specific birth rate by parity is exactly analogous to a crude birth rate by age, the logically prior step. The extreme of sophistication would obviously be an interval-specific, parity-specific, duration-specific, age-specific birth rate: a rate that indicated how many children had been born at one point in time to a group of women of the same age who had been married for the same length of time and who had had the same number of children at the same intervals. This would be an extremely useful dependent variable to have, since it holds all variables except one constant in the demographic set, and enables one to range out into the non-demographic environment unafraid of not having explored the possible confusions arising from un-measured demographic factors. However, it is a rate that no census yet records, and would thus at the moment have to be very expensively obtained from a fresh sample. The probability of finding any quantity of such women in a sample is obviously small, and illustrates the difficulties with which students of fertility have to contend. As Ryder says, the set of six variables could be feasibly gathered in a governmental system of registra-tion and enumeration, and were they to be, all fertility rates would be derivable from the system of birth rates jointly specific for the six.

2   NATURAL FERTILITY

The basic question, then, in any study in which fertility is the dependent variable, is how many women have how many children over what period of time?   Since it is obviously true that most women do not realise their full reproductive potential, it follows both that the determinants of fertility are best seen as checks and that the first question is therefore how many children *could* a woman have over her reproductive period? Until we can answer this, we cannot know how strong the checks are. Moreover, until we know the biological factors con-tributing to fecundity we shall not be able to interpret properly the checked performance that we in fact observe almost every-where, and in particular, we shall not be able to disentangle these biological factors from social ones.

Several demographers have thus devoted a great deal of energy to the calculation of natural fertility rates. A natural fertility rate is not quite the same as fecundity rate. Fecundity is a function of viable ovulation and ejaculation, fertilisation and nidation. Necessary, however, for the unit which contributes to a fertility measure (a birth) are embryonic nurture and the live birth itself. The probability of achieving these steps may vary from zero to one: there may be copulation without ovulation or ejaculation; ovulation without conception; and conception without birth. The probabilities will be affected by both social and biological factors. A theoretical fecundity rate would be of interest to biologists, who could match it against observed socially-unregulated fertility rates. Demographers and sociologists are interested in comparing the latter with socially-regulated ones. Hence the considerable concern with natural fertility.

An understanding of the ways in which calculations of natural fertility are made, the sorts of information that are necessary and the kinds of assumptions that have to be made, is essential if one is to appreciate properly the observed fertility of any population. Such calculations, however, take one immediately into areas not usually familiar to sociologists, and so rather than interrupt this chapter with an excursion into the minutiae of natural fertility, I have discussed them in the Appendix. Here, I proceed on the basis of an extremely useful synthesis prepared by Bourgeois-Pichat, leaving an examination of the analytical components of the synthesis to that Appendix.

Bourgeois-Pichat (1965a; 1965b) has calculated the likely rate of live births per year of marriage by age for a population not practising deliberate birth control. His calculations also take account of the modern revisions of gross fecundity and foetal mortality, now both believed to be higher than thought earlier. In a population of married women between 20 and 24, whose coital frequency is 8 per cycle, who experience a delay of conception (independent of infecund periods and foetal deaths) of 1·90 cycles, whose infecund period (pregnancy plus post-partum infecundity) is 24 cycles and whose interruption from foetal deaths is 5·90 cycles, he calculates that the annual fertility rate would be ·474. The other fertility rates by age are:

TABLE I

Age	15–19	25–29	30–34	35–39	40–44	45–49	50–54
Rate	0·471	0·463	0·441	0·420	0·392	0·371	0·350

Using the much lower estimates of post-partum infecundity adopted, for example, by James,[1] correspondingly higher total rates would be achieved. Clark's (1967) indication of the similarity between Bourgeois-Pichat's calculations and the annual fertility rate of the Hutterites (an anabaptist sect settled in the north-western U.S.A. and the prairie provinces of Canada) is therefore misleading, since calculations made on observations from that society would yield a *higher* rate (James, 1964–5).

Bourgeois-Pichat (1965a) takes the point that calculations of natural fertility are likely to vary between societies with variations in particular social and biological parameters (and thus that the search for *one* rate of natural fertility is likely to be fruitless), and presents a typology of 280 logically possible types of natural fertility. He arrives at this total by distinguishing eight types of fertility, seven types of sterility and five types of marriage pattern. The first eight are as follows:

TABLE II

Coital frequency by cycle, women 20–24	All ovulations fecundable		1/4 ovulations fecundable	
	Temporary sterility*			
	Long	*Short*	*Long*	*Short*
8	a_L	a_S	b_L	b_S
12	A_L	A_S	B_L	B_S

*Short temporary sterility: 1 cycle after birth; long temporary sterility: 14 cycles after birth (from Henry, 1964; Dandekar, 1959).

The seven types of distribution of permanent sterility range from 38·2 per cent for women aged 20–24 recorded for the Caribbean to the very low figure of 2·5 per cent calculated from the demographic information available on the early eighteenth-century French Canadians. The five types of marriage are similarly distributed, and range from the low marriage age and large proportion married of Africa south of the Sahara to the relatively high marriage age and low pro-

[1]Fuller references on natural fertility appear in the Appendix.

portion married of Latin America and Europe (the former having a rather higher average age at marriage but a lower survival rate through marriage than the latter).[2] I have already described his conclusions for the a_L populations. The comparable figures for the others (at ages 20–24) are: a_S, 0·902; b_L, 0·395; b_S 0·654; A_L, 0·485; A_S, 0·941; B_L, 0·426; and B_S, 0·243. a_S and A_S are theoretical possibilities, on the crucial assumptions of constantly fecund ovulations and a post-partum infecund period of only one cycle, and do not appear to have existed. Bourgeois-Pichet can, however, fit his other six types to observed populations, and does so in graph 5 of his article. The fits are by no means perfect, but close enough to accept that his logic is appropriate for discovering the possibilities for natural fertility in various populations. To date, however, he has not calculated the natural fertility rates for all of the 280 theoretically possible combinations.

Nevertheless, his results enable one to make some preliminary comparisons. Taking the a_L category in his eight-fold typology of types of fertility (one which, it will be recalled, is relatively conservative in its assumptions), and ignoring for the moment the distribution of permanent sterility and the types of marriage, it is possible to calculate expected completed family sizes for a population in which women are married early, complete their fecund period and practice no deliberate birth control. Assuming the period at risk of conception is thirty years, and taking Bourgeois-Pichat's average annual natural fertility of 0·443, the expected family size is 13·248. This, it must be emphasised, makes no allowance for women not completing their fecund period, for some women getting married later, or for infant mortality. Bearing these reservations in mind, the correspondence between the expected figure of 13·2 and observed total fertilities is not too bad. It is better if one takes Sauvy's (1961) slightly lower estimate of 10–12 for white populations (Asian ones, for example, rarely living out the full fecund period). Hutterites born between 1896 and 1905 displayed an average total fertility of 10·6 (Eaton and Mayer, 1953);[3] French

[2]The crucial importance of marriage patterns in accounting for fertility rates is discussed below.

[3]In Bourgeois-Pichat's terms, the Hutterites in fact fall nearer the a_S or A_S end of the distribution than to the a_L or A_L end. One would thus expect an even higher total fertility (a point that Clark (1967) overlooks).

Candians married between 1666 and 1681, 9·0, and married under 20 and recorded in 1941, 9·9 (Lorimer, 1954). A mode of more than 13 for women over 65 in 1941 was recorded in French Canada.

Given the reservations that I have just made, no immediate conclusions can be drawn from the much lower figures for almost all other populations. The difference between the expected value of 10–14 and the recorded value of, for example, 3·29 for women married under the age of 20 and whose marriages had lasted for 30 to 34 years in England and Wales in 1961 may not necessarily *all* be attributable to deliberate family limitation. In this case, however, where health conditions are good, it is likely that such an inference is safer than it would be, say, for the 8·8 recorded for comparable Brazilian women. Until more information is provided within the kind of framework set out by Bourgeois-Pichat, a framework that encompasses most detailed research work on natural fertility, we cannot be certain just how much variance can be attributed to deliberate limitation, and thus just how much variance needs sociological explanation. There is, however, no doubt about the essential usefulness of calculations of natural fertility.

Earlier, I said that the basic question in any study in which fertility is the dependent variable is: how many women have how many children over what period of time? Since in most cases we cannot afford to wait for couples to complete their families, this remains as the first question. But precisely because we cannot wait, there has to be this intricate ingenuity in devising measures that approximate as nearly as possible the ideal of completed family size. This qualification does not apply, of course, to historical populations, but the drawback with these is usually that registration is so poor that a disproportionate amount of effort has to be devoted to actually reconstructing the demographic tendencies before any explanation is attempted.

3 IDEAL, DESIRED AND EXPECTED FERTILITY

Ultimately, we want to measure actual reproductive performance, and especially completed cohort fertility, and it is to these that the measures already discussed refer. However, just as a great deal of information can be obtained from a comparison of theoretical natural fertility rates and actual fertility, so there is a lot to be gained from comparing ideal, desired and expected family sizes with each other and with performance.

Some time ago, Stoetzel (1955) noticed that European fertility ideals exceeded actual performance. The same situation, with higher ideals and higher actual fertility, prevailed in the United States (Freedman, Goldberg and Sharp, 1955). The more recent European situation can be gauged from the evidence compiled by Glass in two papers (1962; 1968), and the more recent American state of affairs in this respect has been the subject of an intensive field study and subsequent investigations (Freedman, Whelpton and Campbell, 1959; Whelpton, Campbell and Patterson, 1966; Ryder and Westoff, 1967). Judith Blake has documented the changes in ideal family size in the United States (1966).

Stoetzel observed that whereas European ideals were characteristically somewhere between two and three children, actual completed family size when projected to the end of the child-bearing period fell below this, at about two. Glass's evidence, however, demonstrates that for couples married more recently, the actual fertility is rising to meet the ideals more closely, although the ideals themselves have not changed.[4]

The Michigan Growth of American Families Study (Freedman *et al*, 1959; Whelpton *et al*, 1966) examined 'the number of children the wives considered ideal for the average American family, the number they said they themselves would have if they could live their lives again under ideal conditions, the number they wanted under their actual and anticipated circumstances, and the number they expected.' The main purpose of the two studies, made on samples in 1955 and 1960, was to test the reliability of fertility expectations. The most detailed report on the relationship between these various variables appears in the second report. There, it appears that for all couples (white and non-white, where the wife's age was between 18 and 39) the ideal was 3·4 and 3·5, the number desired if life could be relived, between 3·6 and 3·7, the number desired at the time of interview, between 3·1 and 3·4, and the number

[4]Differentials between and within societies are discussed in more detail in Chapters IV and V.

actually expected, between 2·8 and 3·5 (the most likely being 3·1). It was one of the findings of the G.A.F. research that expectations in the aggregate corresponded extraordinarily well with actual fertility when the 1955 and 1960 samples were compared, and the expectations reported above for the 1960 sample can therefore—for the purposes of my argument here—be taken to be equivalent to actual fertility. It is clear that the mid-1950s situation, now vanished in Europe, still pertains in the United States. Such a state of affairs immediately raises interesting comparative sociological questions (as do comparisons within the G.A.F. sample and within and between European societies), and illustrates the value of these measures as dependent variables.

No such sophisticated data are available for developing countries where, for practical reasons alone, information on couples' ideals, desires and expectations is even more crucial. Nevertheless there is now a large body of information of varying quality on ideal or desired family size for various developing societies which can be matched with reproductive performances. Very broadly, most couples in these societies want about four children, and have more. In Japan alone of those of which an intensive study has been reported, do ideals exceed performance as they do in the West, but then Japan can hardly be considered a developing country by most indicators. There is a suggestion that younger age-groups in a few scattered societies such as Thailand and Turkey are now in the Western situation, but the suggestion is not strong enough to quash disputes as to whether or not current trends indicate a general lowering of ideals (Mauldin, 1965a; Berelson, 1966; Davis, 1967). In no developing society has an attempt yet been made to test the reliability of aggregate birth expectations for predicting fertility.

4 THE QUALITY OF THE DATA

By comparison with other social sciences, demography and thus population studies are well-supplied with data. By any absolute standard, however, they are not. Even the censuses of the most advanced countries do not provide the information necessary to calculate certain specific fertility rates, and, as Mauldin illustrates (1965b), much of the data on ideals, desires and expectations is not comparable because of the lack of comparability between questionnaires. However, Ryder puts the quality of data on fertility into perspective for sociologists. 'The analysis of fertility requires good measures not only of its dependent variables but also of the independent variables with which they may be interrelated. The sophistication of measurement of the former is clearly far in advance of that achieved in those fields which have major definitional responsibility for the latter.'[5]

[5]Only after this chapter was completed was I able to see the results of some of Ryder's further work (1969), in which he refines still further the measures of cohort fertility, such that he is able to distinguish more than has hitherto been possible the relative contribution of total quantity and timing of the critical variables.

CHAPTER III

Associated Factors

In all parts of that indeterminate area called 'sociology', there are vigorous disputes about the proper strategies of enquiry. The study of the social determinants of fertility is no exception, but the arguments here are less extensive. This because there is not, and logically cannot be, much dispute about the intervening variables that one must look at. Presented with a fertility rate, however defined, the first questions are: for how long are what proportion of women in the population exposed to the risk of conception? and, within this period, what measures are taken to encourage or reduce that risk? Lying behind these questions in turn are those which attempt to find out why these periods and measures should be as they are. This chapter is devoted to the first of these two sets of questions.

In what has come to be regarded as a classic article, Davis and Blake (1956) have classified what they term the 'intermediate variables' in the following way:

Factors affecting exposure to intercourse ('Intercourse variables'):

(*a*) Those governing the formation and dissolution of unions in the reproductive period.

   (i) Age of entry into sexual unions.

   (ii) Permanent celibacy: proportion of women never entering sexual unions.

   (iii) Amount of reproductive period spent after or between unions.

      (*a*) When unions are broken by divorce, separation or desertion.

      (*b*) When unions are broken by death of husband.

(*b*) Those governing the exposure to intercourse within unions.

   (iv) Voluntary abstinence.

18

(v) Involuntary abstinence (from impotence, illness, unavoidable but temporary separations).

(vi) Coital frequency (excluding periods of abstinence).

(c) Factors affecting exposure to conception ('Conception variables'):

(vii) Fecundity or infecundity, as affected by involuntary causes.

(viii) Use or non-use of contraception.
    (a) By mechanical and chemical means.
    (b) By other means.

(ix) Fecundity or infecundity, as affected by voluntary causes (sterilisation, subincision, medical treatment, etc.).

(d) Factors affecting gestation and successful parturition ('Gestation variables'):

(x) Foetal mortality from involuntary causes.

(xi) Foetal mortality from voluntary causes.

Davis and Blake point out that different combinations of values for these factors could produce identical fertility rates, and that, conversely, similar values on many could still produce different rates. Moreover, many of these means of increasing or reducing fertility can be implemented unintentionally, as the result of pursuing some other purpose.

I have discussed (vi), (vii) and (x) in dealing with calculations of natural fertility in the Appendix. The remaining eight, more familiarly understood as marriage, abstinence, contraception (including sterilisation) and abortion, are the subject of this chapter.

1 MARRIAGE
(a) *In General*

It is immediately obvious from the calculations that I described in the previous chapter that age at marriage, and proportions married, in a population of women is a fundamental determinant of fertility in a society. Bourgeois-Pichat (1965a) has distinguished five types of marriage from census data taken from the period between 1926 (the only reliable census in the U.S.S.R. before 1959) and 1961:

TABLE III

Proportions married in each age-group

	15–19	20–24	25–29	30–34	35–39	40–44	45–49	50–54
Type 1 ..	60	92	95	95	95	87	83	70
Type 2 ..	30	75	88	88	86	78	70	50
Type 3 ..	35	80	92	92	90	85	72	60
Type 4 ..	20	55	70	75	75	70	65	60
Type 5 ..	5	45	70	80	80	80	75	70

Source: Bourgeois-Pichat (1965a).

The first type is derived from figures on five societies only, all from Africa south of the Sahara; the second from four societies in North Africa; the third from nine societies in Asia; the fourth from twelve societies in Latin America (including the Caribbean); and the fifth from 21 societies, mostly European but including Australia, New Zealand, the U.S.A. and the U.S.S.R. Making no allowance for mortality before the end of the fecund period, it can be easily calculated that a woman from the first type has, on average, a married life expectancy of 33·9 years; from the second type, 30·3; from the third, 27·8; from the fourth, 25·0; and from the fifth, 24·5. As Bourgeois-Pichat himself concludes, 'all other things being equal, Latin America and Europe only use 60 per cent of their potential, whereas Africa south of the Sahara uses 85 per cent of its potential. But 'all other things being equal' puts everything into question.' They are not equal, and in many cases serve to effectively counteract the demographic influence of early and universal marriage.[1] The most important of these influences is, of course, mortality.

[1]Sociologists will be aware that the description " marriage " covers a multitude of domestic arrangements in which men and women cohabit and reproduce. The Latin American figures in particular are deflated by an indeterminate amount as a result of the widespread prevalence of " consensual unions ", *de facto* but often not *de jure* stable unions. See Mortara (1961) ; Blake (1961) ; Braithwaite and Roberts (1961).

The differences between these five types are clear. However, by contrast with one crucial historical pattern of nuptiality, all five represent a situation of relatively universal marriage, and relatively universal early marriage at that. The historical case is that of the so-called 'European' marriage pattern, more exactly the pattern that prevailed in northern and Western Europe from about the sixteenth century to the fourth decade of the twentieth. Hajnal, who has explored the history of the European marriage pattern in some detail (1965), illustrates its divergence from the non-European pattern with the following simple comparison:

TABLE IV

Selected European countries in 1900: percentages of women married at selected ages

	20–24	25–29	45–49
Belgium	29	59	83
Sweden	20	48	81
Bulgaria	76	97	99
Serbia	84	98	99

Source: Hajnal (1965), adapted.

The similarity between the Bulgarian and Serbian rates and those that Bourgeois-Pichat compiles for the first three of his types is immediately obvious. Almost equally clear is the change that has overtaken the European pattern in the past fifty years or so.

As I have already said, the theoretical relationship between age at marriage and marital fertility is a simple one (see Coale, 1965; Cole, 1965). However, as Bourgeois-Pichat emphasises, the relationship is only simple in practice on the basis of a set of simplifying demographic assumptions. Nevertheless, one would expect a correlation between European marriage and lower marital fertility on the one hand, and non-European marriage and higher marital fertility on the other. It exists. Hajnal provides some brief illustrative evidence. More detailed information comes, for example, in

Wrigley's (1966a) reconstruction of nuptiality and natality for the village of Colyton in Devon in the late sixteenth, seventeenth and early eighteenth centuries. Before 1646, the average age at marriage for women was about 27, extremely late by any standards, and after the terrible mortality of that year, rose to 30. Given the relatively high 'ordinary' mortality (Wrigley, 1968) and the fact that in pre-industrial European populations almost all women appear to have finished bearing children by the age of 40, with very probably a rapid fall in fecundity in their thirties, it is clear that the effect of such a change in nuptiality would have a dramatic effect on natality. It did, and Wrigley documents the extent to which it did. Unfortunately for my immediate purpose, the figures are confounded by the fact that there appears to have been greater control of fertility *within* marriage after 1646, but it is nevertheless certain that the rising age at marriage must have had a considerable effect on fertility. By taking the average completed family size of *all* women married over 30 in Colyton between 1560 and 1837 (thus lessening the effect of the post–1646 marriage cohorts with their severe birth control, a severity that lasted until about 1720), which is 2·5, and comparing this with the mean number of children ever born to women married under the age of 13 and still alive at the age of 35 in Nagpur District in Bombay State, as recorded by Driver (1963), which is 6·6, the point comes out clearly. The prevalence of the European marriage pattern almost certainly had a great effect on fertility in pre-industrial northern and western Europe from the sixteenth or seventeenth centuries, and this effect continued somewhat abated through into the 1940s.

The European marriage pattern appeared first at the beginning of the seventeenth century, and apparently first in the highest social classes (Henry, 1956; Henry and Levy, 1960; Hollingsworth, 1957; 1964). Records for all groups other than the aristocracy or the high bourgeoisie before this period are, of course, very poor indeed, but such evidence as can be adduced suggests that in medieval northern and western Europe this marriage pattern was more similar to the so-called 'non-European' pattern, more similar, that is, to the developing countries today (with the possible exception of

parts of Latin America). As well as looking at what medieval
evidence he can find, and disputing one long-standing argument that the age at marriage in medieval Britain was relatively high, Hajnal (1965) reviews the material for the ancient
world. Marriage there too seems to have been early and relatively universal. Hopkins (1964–65) has suggested that over
50 per cent of the daughters of the respectable classes in Rome
(those of whom records were left behind in the form of literary
evidence from their status-equals and tombstone inscriptions)
were married by the age of 15.

Taking the information on the historical European marriage
pattern (information which is still distressingly sparse) together
with a classification of modern marriage patterns of the kind
provided by Bourgeois–Pichat, it is possible to distinguish
three broad groups. At one extreme is pre-industrial northern
and western Europe, at the other black Africa, and in between,
and gradually approaching the second rather than the first,
modern industrial societies. The continuing decline in marriage rates of a 'European' type is well illustrated from the
detailed commentary provided for England and Wales by the
Registrar General in his *Statistical Review* for 1965 (General
Register Office, annual: 1965, III, published 1968).

For the purposes of the sociology of fertility, it is a sad irony
that those societies for which we have the most comprehensive,
detailed and subtle sociological descriptions, the primitive
ones, are also those for which we have the least demographic
information. With a small handful of creditable exceptions,
social anthropologists have not been given to collecting
statistics, or to collecting data over any period of time, and
both are necessary for a demographic picture. Moreover,
colonial administrations only gathered enough crude aggregate figures to meet their immediate practical needs. Most
disappointing of all is the fact that it is now too late to gather
this information. We shall remain forever ignorant of the
detailed demography of small-scale, pre-literate societies.

However, Nag (1962) took what demographic data he could
find in the Yale Human Relations Area Files for pre-industrial,
including primitive, societies, and attempted inter-correlations
to determine the relative influence of various biological and
social factors on fertility. In only eleven societies did he find

enough evidence to suggest that the age at marriage had a significantly adverse effect on fertility, and five of these societies can hardly be classed as 'primitive'. Carr–Saunders (1922), searching through the secondary literature available to him, can only add four to this list and one more which Nag rejects. [2] It seems, therefore, to be true that in almost all primitive societies there is or was a pattern of early and almost universal marriage. A considerable amount of information still awaits someone prepared to go systematically through the numerous anthropological monographs, but further work is unlikely, in the absence of detailed statistical time series, to indicate the relative causal importance of marriage patterns on fertility in these societies. One can only assume that high and early marriage encouraged fertility. The pattern must have been generally very similar to that of the modern black African states, perhaps the most primitive societies in the modern world.

At some point, there was a transition in northern and western Europe from the non-European pattern of nuptiality to what I have described as the 'European' one. Whether this transition was relatively sudden or whether, as seems more likely, it took place over one or two hundred years, there is no doubt that it had some effect on fertility. Much more recently, indeed within the past thirty years, the pattern has reverted to the older one, with younger ages at marriage and a greater proportion of women married. These changes indicate the relevance of marriage patterns to discussions of the so-called 'demographic transition', and in order to make the rest of the discussion in this chapter intelligible, it is necessary to discuss this notion.

(b) *In the Demographic Transition*

Since Landry described what he called the 'demographic revolution' in 1934, demographers, sociologists and economic historians have debated the existence and nature of a general pattern of transition from a state of high birth and death rates

[2]Nag's eleven are: Nguni, Havasupai, Sioux, Walapai, Kgatla, Dusan and, less obviously 'primitive', Hutterite, Puerto Rico, China, Taiwan and Barbados. It is surprising that given his wide brief, he did not include agricultural Europe from 1600 to 1900. Carr–Saunders adds Eskimo (which Nag rejects), Shushwap, Lillooet, Tehuelche and Abipone.

to a state of low birth and death rates. It has been most usually asserted that the transition begins when the mortality rate falls, leaving a high fertility rate unchecked and thus leading the society towards a situation of rapid growth and heavy pressure on resources. Eventually, survival demands that the fertility of the population in question falls to meet the reduced mortality. The transition is then completed.

I am not concerned, in this chapter, with the merits and demerits of this bold generalisation. Suffice it to say that, like most generalisations in social science, it is open to a great deal of doubt and modification. Much of the debate about it centres around the question of whether in fact mortality always declines first, whether a drop in fertility rates is seen as a response to the threat raised by lowered mortality, and whether fertility is the only such response. The last two questions to be asked at all clearly demand an affirmative answer to the one before them. Nevertheless, fertility has declined in very many societies, and since this is the case, it is essential to find out how it has done so: has it been as a result of a rise in the age at marriage and a change in the proportions marrying, or has it been rather the result of greater control of fertility within marriage? Or has it been something of both?

From what I have already said, it is clear that there was the beginnings of a demographic transition in northern and western Europe somewhere towards the end of the medieval period. The age at marriage rose and fewer women married. This almost certainly served to reduce fertility, although there is no evidence that it was intended to do so, in the absence of which there is dispute (Hajnal, 1965; Hollingsworth, 1964; van de Walle, 1968). As a step to describing the various mechanisms of transition, Matras (1965a) has outlined a typology of what he calls 'strategies of family formation':

TABLE V

	Uncontrolled fertility	*Controlled fertility*
Early marriage	Strategy A	Strategy B
Late marriage	Strategy C	Strategy D

Source: Matras (1965a).

Most societies are still at the stage of strategy A, in which 'uncontrolled fertility' should be taken in a relative sense. In the sixteenth century or perhaps a little before, the populations of northern and western Europe moved from A to C. White colonial societies have tended to move from A to B (see, for instance, Potter, 1965; Coale and Zelnik, 1963; Yasuba, 1962). Japan, uniquely, has moved straight across from A to D, the most drastic transition of all (Tauber, 1958; Davis, 1963). Wrigley's evidence for Colyton suggests a move from C to D and back to C again, before industrialisation. The European societies which did not experience the drop in nuptiality in the sixteenth century have also gone from A to B, the same path along which international agencies and anxious health ministries are now trying to force many modern developing societies. The other European societies, discussed by Hajnal, have moved from C to B, although by different paths.

In a superbly compressed account of the transition to low fertility, Coale (1967) has suggested a neat formula for calculating the relative contribution of changes in the proportions married and marital fertility to the decline of fertility,[3] and also summarised those social and economic factors conventionally believed to have had something to do with the transition. Coale concludes the first part of his paper by tentatively suggesting that if there is any common demographic characteristic of the transition, it is that populations abandon strategy C for D, and then move to B once birth control within marriage has become effective enough for their purposes. He adds that this would seem particularly plausible in view of the rather unnatural nature of the European marriage pattern C: couples revert to earlier marriage once they are less anxious about excess fertility.

The path of transition characteristic of the white colonies or ex-colonies and modern developing societies, from A to B, raises questions about birth control within marriage rather than about control through marriage, and as such is relevant to the later discussion in this chapter. However, several demographers have devoted energy to calculating if, and if so to what extent, a rise in the age at marriage in developing

[3] The formula is described in the bibliographical note to Coale's paper.

societies might reinforce the fertility decline induced by widespread contraception. Das (1967) looked at the marital fertility rates in Mysore, Madras and Kerala, and matched them against the prevalent age at marriage in each of the states to see if there was any connection. In Mysore, about 93 per cent of the women in the age group 15–24 are married,[4] in Madras about 75 per cent, and in Kerala, only about 57 per cent. One would therefore expect marital fertility to be highest in Mysore and lowest in Kerala. It is indeed highest in Mysore, if only by a small margin, but the fertility rate in Kerala is higher than that in Madras. It seems that the timing of births is simply postponed in the southern state, and that the number is not reduced by a higher age at marriage. Das is thus pessimistic about the likely effects of a rise in the age at marriage on Indian fertility, suggesting that marriage must be postponed to a very late age for it to affect fertility to any significant extent. Agarwala (1967), however, has calculated that a rise in the average age at marriage in India from 15·6 years to the Kerala average of 19·3 would dampen marital fertility by between 21 and 29 per cent. His assumption is that it would be thirty years before couples marrying later adjusted their fertility back up the old levels, by which time hopefully contraception within marriage would have taken hold in India and thus prevented such a return. This approach is clearly more sophisticated than Das's, but the crucial assumption remains, as far as I am aware, untested. The question is therefore open to doubt. The inversion of the expected relationship between Madras and Kerala suggests that age at marriage is of slender importance in affecting Indian marital fertility, and indeed some sociological evidence, which I discuss later, suggests that it is the type of *kinship* organisation within which the marriage takes place rather than the *age* at which it takes place which is the determining factor.

I said that the transition in the white colonial and ex-colonial territories was from A to B. This is only the most tentative of tentative generalisations, since historical work on them is still scarce. It is certainly true that, for example, Beshers' (1967) simple assumption that the decline in fertility

---

[4]The approximation results from the fact that the official figures are unreliable, and that surveys give slightly different results.

3

which started in the United States in the first decades of the nineteenth century was entirely due to the increasing practice of contraception rests on the slenderest of evidence. There is some suggestion that the age at marriage rose from the phenomenally low levels at which it rested in the colonial period, particularly in the towns (Potter, 1965).

However, Japan's transition from A to D is much better documented, presumably because it presents a dramatic combination of extraordinarily rapid economic growth after the Meiji Restoration in 1868 and an at first equally startling population increase followed by a no less startling decline in the rate of growth. The gross reproduction rate more than halved between 1925 and 1955, from 2·6 to 1·2. The Japanese have achieved this decline by migration, abortion, contraception, sterilisation and a rise in the age at marriage perhaps faster than that recorded for any other society at any other time. In 1920, 68·6 per cent of the women in the 20–24 age group were married, in 1940 the proportion had dropped to 46·5, and in 1955 to 33·9 (Tauber, 1958). By the age of 30, though, as many Japanese women are married as ever, and indeed the proportion of women never married in the age group of 40–44 is lower in Japan than in any other industrial country. Davis (1963) suggests that this may be a reflection of the old marriage pattern in which unions were arranged by the parents, and that Japan will come up to meet the other advanced societies as the vestiges of this old social organisation vanish. There is little doubt that Japan is still in a state of transition, although the most dramatic period seems to be over now.

Colyton, as I said, appeared to move from 1560 to 1837 from C to D and back to C again (Wrigley, 1966a). Like almost all pre-industrial European societies, this small cell has now no doubt moved across to B, a state of relatively early marriage and effective control of fertility within it. But before discussing the general move that most northern and western European societies made from C to B, it is worth looking at one of the demographically most remarkable, and most tragic, societies of all: Ireland. Ireland was hit more severely than any other north-western European society by the potato blight of the mid-1840s, largely becaue it was more dependent on this vegetable than other affected countries, such as the Netherlands. Up to the most severe period of famine, in 1845–48, Ireland had moved slightly from the classic marriage pattern of northern and western Europe precisely as a result of the introduction of the potato. This enabled families to survive on somewhat smaller holdings, since its yield was greater than other traditional crops, and so enabled families to establish themselves rather earlier. Just how far the age at marriage did drop in eighteenth-century Ireland is a matter for dispute (Connell, 1950; Glass, 1953; Drake, 1963; Hajnal, 1965). In any event, the blight was an utter disaster. Perhaps two million died, two million emigrated, and the remaining four million reverted to a drastic version of the European marriage pattern, marrying late and leaving a large number of unmarried people through into the non-fecund period. The birth rate fell, but less quickly and to less low levels than in neighbouring England and Wales, where the institutional environment was more conducive to the introduction of methods of birth control in marriage. And unlike, for instance, Sweden, Ireland had no recourse to a high illegitimacy rate, again a function of its peculiar culture. What is demographically interesting about Ireland is that it demonstrates the relative ineffectiveness of a later age at marriage and a larger proportion unmarried as against contraception and abortion as regulators of marital fertility. The practical implication is simple. If any society wishes to reduce its marital fertility, the postponement of marriage on even such a drastic (and, one might argue, socially demoralising) scale as practised by the Irish will be less efficient and humane than encouraging contraception and abortion within marriage.

Historical demographers and economic historians, but unfortunately neither other historians nor sociologists, have recently begun to look more closely at the mechanism of transition from C to B in the (more advanced) societies that went through their demographic transition from between the end of the eighteenth century and the end of the nineteenth. Returning to Matras' schematic description of the four logically possible strategies, it is clear that the transition from C to B can be direct, or through A, or, as Coale suggests, through D. It is of course unlikely that any national society will show a clean transition along any one of these paths. Davis' recent exposition of a more sophisticated, so-called 'multiphasic' model of demographic response at the beginning of the period of transition (Davis, 1963) illustrates the point that societies are more likely to take several demographic steps at once, and that there will be variations between different regions and different social groups within the nation.

Matras himself (1965b; 1965–66) has looked at the change in strategies in Scandinavia, Britain and the United States. The evidence for the first two is not conclusive, but in so far as it reveals anything it indicates a move from C through strategy D, rather than through A or directly to B, and thus supports Coale. Demeny (1968a), examining the situation in Austria–Hungary between 1880 and 1910, also found that the move was through D, although there was a hint from the German-speaking parts of Austria that the age at marriage had begun to decline before marital fertility did so. Van de Walle (1968), looking at France, Belgium, the Netherlands and Switzerland, also found conflicting evidence (which he does not clearly resolve), but concludes that the pattern was very probably a direct transition from C to B, passing through neither A nor D. Add to this the fact that Matras finds inter-esting intra-societal differences, by education and industry-group of the husband, and that Demeny finds a multitude of different combinations of nuptiality and natality in the fertility decline in the Hapsburg Empire, and it is clear that the more research is done, the less confident must any general descrip-tion of the mechanics of the transition be. Coale's hypothesis that the development of birth control within marriage has released the natural tendency for early marriage in European populations is not yet fully substantiated. Van de Walle, indeed, considers this to be *a priori* unlikely, but it does account for *some* of the evidence. However, discussions of why such a change did or did not take place are the subject of a later chapter. Meanwhile, more research on the mechanism in various societies and groups will have to be done.

(c) The Interruption and Dissolution of Unions
There is a fair amount of information on the effects on marital fertility of Davis and Blake's third variable: the amount of the

reproductive period spent after or between unions, either as a result of divorce, separation or desertion, or as a result of the husband's death. The Registrar General's reports on fertility in Britain (see, for example, General Register Office, 1966) indicate the fertility of remarried women as a ratio of the fertility of women who have only married once. Obviously, it is generally lower, although by how much depends on the length and fertility of the earlier marriage, the time between the marriages, and the proportion of the fecund period that both marriages together cover. Blake (1961) estimated that women living in unstable unions in Jamaica fell below their expected fertility (if the unions had been continuous) by 27 per cent. Moreover, she considers that her sample considerably under-represented conjugal instability in the Jamaican population. Nag (1962) found evidence of a negative effect of the absence of the spouse on fertility in eleven societies. However, little faith can be placed in this figure. He does not include either Barbados or Jamaica, although they are in his sample, and by the time that he was writing the structure and effects of marital relations in the Carribbean were widely known. And although he reports the Yapese of the north-western Pacific as one of his eleven, a detailed independent study carried out several years before he wrote (see Lorimer, 1954) was firm in concluding that the frequent absence of male Yapese during their wives' fecund period had no effect either way on their wives' fertility. Moreover, he certainly ignored some societies in which divorce or more informal separation does badly affect births. Ardener (1962) has recently shown such a situation among the Bakweri in Nigeria.

All the societies except three (Dinka, Nguni and Hutterite) that Nag reports as ones in which a high proportion of widows reduces marital fertility are Asian, and it has long been assumed that the taboos on widow re-marriage in the Indian sub-continent had such an effect. Driver's (1963) detailed study of Nagpur, however, has rather given the lie to this belief. He found that even when age was held constant, the fertility of widows *exceeded* that of married women. What appeared to have happened was that the very fertile widowed women had almost no chance of remarrying, but that those women widowed (a large proportion, given the high mortality in India) who were less fertile did remarry, thus removing themselves from the population of the still-widowed. Driver estimated, from his sample, that a woman with six or more children by the time that she is widowed has only a 1 in 52 chance of marrying again, whereas a woman widowed with a smaller family has a much greater probability, rising to 20 in 23 for the infertile. It is, therefore, likely that widowhood in India has a similar statistical effect to divorce and separation in Europe or the West Indies, removing women only temporarily from the risk of conception, unless they already have a high parity, in which case the fertility rate will not have been affected anyway.

Similar considerations probably apply in other societies, but there is that small number of modern societies where the male population has suffered disproportionate mortality, with the result that women—whatever their parity so far—just cannot find men to re-marry. Such a state of affairs will also, of course, affect the rate of first marriages. The classic, and terrible, example of this situation in the twentieth century is the Soviet Union. Estimates of population loss since the October Revolution vary (Lorimer, 1946; Brackett, 1962; Heer, 1968; Petersen, 1961), but it would appear that 8 million were lost in the fighting between 1916 and 1918, 5 million in the famine between 1921 and 1923, 10 million during collectivisation (this is Stalin's own estimate!) and between 12 and 19 million in the 'Great Patriotic War'. The birth deficits produced by this appalling mortality, which disproportionately affected men, are very high indeed, and one estimate puts the total population loss in Russia during the Soviet period at 80 million. This is probably an exaggeration, but it would not seem that the loss was less than 55 million, despite the attempts to compensate by intermittent pro-natalist programmes.

(d) Polygyny and Polyandry

Polygyny is one solution to this state of affairs, and although not practised in Russia, is prevalent in some primitive societies. There is, however, little evidence and much dispute about whether it increases or reduces fertility (Nag, 1962; Lorimer, 1954). Kirk (1967) considers that polygyny is now rare in Moslem countries, and that where it does occur it is probably the response to the infertility or sub-fertility of the first wife. Polyandry is much rarer, and Nag found no difference in the fertility of polyandrously and non-polyandrously married women among the Toda and the Jaunsari, the two societies that he investigated from the data on them in the Yale files.

2 COITAL FREQUENCY

I have already dealt with the evidence, such as it is, on coital frequencies within marriage in the discussion of natural fertility. No monograph evidence exists, to my knowledge, to reduce the uncertainty, so that alternative assumptions of a frequency of eight per cycle for the developing societies and twelve for others still stand (Bourgeois–Pichat, 1965a; 1965b). Equally, there is no useful information on abstinence. It is unlikely that abstinence within marriage, as distinct from permanent celibacy or intermittent restraint through *coitus interruptus, reservatus,* or other sexual diversions, has ever had any significant impact on marital fertility.

3 BIRTH CONTROL

Much more important in limiting such fertility has been the adoption of some particular contraceptive technique, although it is still not clear whether, in view of the information that is coming to light on abortion rates (see discussion of Freedman, 1966, p. 48 below), such techniques are mainly responsible for fertility control in most societies. Contraception can be realised by a variety of methods, separately or together; use of the so-called 'safe period', rubber penis sheaths, vaginal caps, douches, jellies, creams, suppositories, foam tablets, sponges, tampons, coils, loops, orally-induced chemicals and various sexual positions and styles that avoid insemination. The variety is impressive. In addition there are those voluntary practices, such as male or female sterilisation, subincision, etc. which impair fecundity.

(a) *In Pre-Industrial Societies*

From what I have already said about the mechanisms of

demographic transition, it is clear that such practices are a crucial variable in accounting for them. Carlsson (1966) has recently summarised the elements of the conventional hypothesis about the role of contraception in this transition. 'First, there is a strong tendency to regard birth control, especially contraception, as a recent invention, as something essentially new in human culture. Even if its long history is acknowledged, it is assumed that these methods were not widely used before the nineteenth century (Himes, 1936). The innovation perspective will appear more natural if this were true, so that the decline of fertility started in a setting where there was no, or at most very limited, previous practice of birth control. The theory stresses the importance of the spread of information about contraception and perhaps abortion. Another and most important element is the assumption of lags and a 'trickle down' in the spread of skills and attitudes. Diffusion is supposed to start in metropolitan centres, and to reach other urban places with some delay, and rural areas still later. Overlapping with this is the belief that there is a regional factor; certain regions are reached before others, or are quicker to react. There is finally the firmly established belief in class differentials in the timing of the decline and the acceptance of birth control. Middle-class groups are supposed to be leading, manual workers and the farm population lagging'. In short, the extensive and intensive adoption of deliberate contraception in the 'West' is regarded as a classic case of the 'diffusion of innovations', a familiar hypothesis in sociological discussions of change (see, for example, Rogers, 1961; Coleman, Katz and Menzel, 1957). One recent text on population has reinforced this view (Beshers, 1967), regarding the diffusion of contraceptive practice as in turn dependent upon the diffusion of a rational means-end value system of the kind familiar in American theories of development. Banks, whose early work on the fertility decline in the English middle classes in the last quarter of the nineteenth century has given rise to a great deal of diffusionist thinking, still considers (1968) that three factors relevant to what he calls 'the decision to conceive' were absent during previous periods: a conception of techniques to be used instrumentally rather than expressively, information about methods of contraception, and 'the psychological availability, or willingness, to use contraception'. The hypothesis that Carlsson describes is clearly still current.

As Carlsson points out, the thesis raises two questions. Did birth control within marriage exist on any scale before the transition? And did the use of contraception diffuse outward from the 'centres' and downward from the 'tops' of societies? The answer to the first seems to be a cautious 'yes'. The western Pacific island society of the Tikopia has been well described (Firth, 1963; 1959; Borrie, Firth, and Spillius, 1957), and Firth reports that '*coitus interruptus* was expected to be practised by married people after they had had three or four children'. Nag also suggests that several societies in a primitive or pre-industrial state practised contraception, although of course its efficacy and extent are unknown. Carr–Saunders (1922) says that 'there is a general impression that the knowledge of contraceptive methods has only been acquired in modern times. This, however, is not correct . . . [but] generally speaking, . . . it is not until we arrive at the latest period of human history that we find these practices to be of considerable importance'. He is rather coy about describing in detail the methods he finds reported in the literature. It would seem that the Tikopia are the exception rather than the rule in primitive societies. What was undoubtedly the very effective fertility regulator of female subincision, which was practised by some Australian groups (Birdsell, 1953) and apparently still is in parts of West Africa, was only doubtfully intended to reduce fertility. In all events, fertility was predominantly regulated in primitive societies by abortion, infanticide and prolonged lactation.

Direct evidence is equally if not more sparse for the practice of contraception within marriage in pre-industrial Europe. There are, however, several indirect signs. Meuvret (1965) provides one. In the year from May 1694 to April 1695 there was a 'crisis of subsistence' in parts of rural France as a result of high grain prices (themselves a function of a correctly predicted bad harvest that autumn), and Meuvret has shown how it affected births:

TABLE VI

*Indices of births calculated on base 100 representing
the period May 1693—April 1694*

	May 1694—April 1695	May 1695—April 1696
Parish 1	42	129
Parish 2	58	106
Parish 3	53	109
Parish 4	54	167

Source: Meuvret (1965).

Such a postponement may have been due to some physiological impairment in late 1694 and early 1695, but it then becomes difficult to account for the rapid recovery immediately afterwards. The sudden drop and equally abrupt recovery do suggest successful delays of conception.

Before the end of the eighteenth century, however, marital fertility in Crulai—despite periodic fluctuations—does not seem to have fallen below the level that one would expect for a non-contracepting population with normal fecundity[5] (Gautier and Henry, 1958; Henry, 1965). There is evidence from another French village that birth control within marriage might have been practised from soon after 1750 to affect completed family size, but none for such an effect before that date in any of the other rural communities that have been investigated there. Precisely because of this, Meuvret's evidence is absolutely crucial. It suggests that the means of birth control were known and available to these populations before they used them to limit their completed fertility, and thus casts great suspicion on the thesis that fertility was not limited before the period immediately preceding the Revolution because there was no knowledge of contraception. The question must be: why, despite the fact that they knew how to prevent conceptions, or at least births, did these peasants not do so?

[5]Crulai was the first of Meuvret's parishes; Henry has used the data from this village to calculate rates of natural fertility. (See Appendix.)

Further evidence that such information was available before the transition comes from Wrigley's work on Colyton (1966; 1968). Even despite the extraordinarily late age at marriage after the disaster of 1646, the completed family sizes in Colyton were below theoretical natural levels. This may be accounted for by abnormally low fecundity, or high infant (prebaptismal) mortality, or birth control. The first seems unlikely, as it did for Meuvret's parishes; the second appears not to have been true (Wrigley, 1968); and one is thus left with the third. Additional signs of the practise of birth control are, first, the tell-tale earlier age of completion of family building for women married earlier and, second, the abnormally long interval between the penultimate and final birth. '*Coitus interruptus*', Wrigley cautiously concludes, 'may well have been the most important method of family limitation in use in Colyton in the seventeenth and early eighteenth centuries. It was probably widely employed by French populations to secure a lower marital fertility a century later'.

But some French and some English populations were almost certainly using birth control to regulate marital fertility long before this. Henry (1965, from Henry and Levy, 1960) has compared the legitimate fertility of the French peerage married before thirty in the eighteenth century to the arithmetic average of legitimate peasant fertility in comparable groups:

TABLE VII

	Wife's age					
	20–24	*25–29*	*30–34*	*35–39*	*40–44*	*45–49*
Peers (married 1700–95), rates ..	0·226	0·167	0·063	0·018	0·006	0·000
Index (rural figures as 100) ..	54	40	17	6	4	0
Average of 6 sets of rural rates ..	0·420	0·412	0·369	0·282	0·144	0·013

Among the peers, in addition, the age-specific fertility rate decreases with a lower age at marriage, a pattern characteristic of modern contracepting populations and quite the reverse of what prevailed in contemporary peasant villages. Hollingsworth's detailed reconstruction of the demography of the British peerage from the birth cohort of 1550 also reveals early birth control. Fertility was highest for those born between 1575 and 1599, dropped thereafter to two-thirds of this rate in the 1700–24 cohort, then rose again to a new peak in the 1775–99 one, to fall gradually from the middle of the nineteenth century. Hollingsworth infers that birth control within marriage was being effectively practised by the middle of the seventeenth century (1964).

From this still partial evidence, which will doubtless be augmented as the amount of historical demographic research accelerates, there can be little doubt that the first of the diffusionist assumptions is false. Not only was birth control practised when necessary by many pre-industrial European populations, as well as societies such as Tikopia, but it is fallacious to assume that such practice depends in any simple sense upon the diffusion of contraceptive 'knowledge'. Sutter (Bergues *et al*, 1959) has pointed out that *coitus interruptus* (and, one might add, *coitus reservatus*) is not a culturally specific technique, and it requires no propaganda to be disseminated. It is autochthonous, entirely natural. If the famous Tully River blacks of Australia did not connect sexual intercourse with conception and pregnancy,[6] they are probably almost alone among recorded human societies. Once the connection is understood, it does not require the diffusion of Weberian *Zweckrationalität* to think of *interruptus* or *resveratus*.

That it is false to assume that a population will not know about birth control until it hears about it from the source of invention is a proposition that undermines the assumptions behind the second diffusionist contention: namely, that the knowledge and *thus* the practice of contraception trickled down from the tops and outwards from the centres of societies. If there is such a lag between the top and the bottom and the centre and the periphery, it must be explained by another hypothesis. Carlsson himself, to make his point, has looked at

[6]Leach (1967); Spiro (1968).

the Swedish fertility rates by province, and finds that fertility declined simultaneously in seven of the eight rural regions and in Stockholm from 1860 to 1946. Stockholm by no means led the decline. Norrbotten, the large relatively empty northernmost province, is the exception among the eight. Fertility there rose slightly from 1860 to 1890, and only began to decline from 1891. As Carlsson says, this lag has tended to provide grist for the diffusionist mill, but it can plausibly be explained by a higher infant mortality and one or two other factors. And the diffusionists have still to account for the *parallel* decline of Stockholm and the other seven.

It is, however, true that in most Western societies for which there is differential data,[7] family limitation within marriage did start in the higher social classes and, figuratively speaking, 'spread' to lower ones. The British, French and Swiss upper and upper-middle classes all preceded their status inferiors. However, if the premise behind diffusion theory, namely that knowledge of contraception is a function of being told about it (by anyone other than one's family or peers), is incorrect, it would be mistaken to jump to the conclusion that this spread downwards can be accounted for by increasing information in the same way as one accounts for farmers adopting new techniques (Rogers, 1961) or doctors new drugs (Coleman, Katz, and Menzel, 1957). At the very most, it can be conceded that part of the decline in births may have been due to more efficient techniques becoming available during the past 150 years. Before their introduction, we do not and can never know how many couples were unsuccessfully practising *interruptus* and *reservatus*. Against this concession, however, is the powerful point that the introduction and rapidly expanding availability of contraceptives in the nineteenth century is the *result* of pressure for more effective methods of fertility control, and not the cause of increased fertility decline in a simple *deus ex machina* sense. This argument has rarely been considered by historians (but see Banks and Banks, 1964; Glass, 1940).

---

[7]For Britain, see General Register Officer (1917, 1923), Glass (1938), Lewis–Faning (1949), Banks (1954); for France, Bergues *et al* (1960): for the Genevan bourgeoisie, Henry (1956), and Switzerland generally, Mayer (1952).

(b)   *In Industrial Societies*

To discover the strategies that couples have adopted in building their families it is essential to have cohort data. Period
data on the incidence of contraception, for instance, at one
point in time will tell one nothing about the place of such
contraception in the total strategy; and once one begins to
search for the extra information, one is in practice looking for
cohort data. For living couples, this can be collected through
field surveys, and I shall discuss those that have been made
presently. For past cohorts, however, it is almost always the
case that laborious reconstructions have to be made. The
partial exception to this depressing truth is Great Britain.
There is direct information on the practise of birth control
within marriage for all cohorts married since the beginning
of the century (Lewis–Faning, 1949; Rowntree and Pierce,
1961–62; work in progress).[8] In addition, Matras (1965–66)
has made use of the 1911 Census report on fertility and marriage (General Register Office, 1917; 1923), together with
the 1946 Family Census (Glass and Grebenik, 1954) and the
1951 Census Fertility Report to estimate the number of controllers over the period from the latter quarter of the nineteenth century.

Matras' estimates of the use of birth control within marriage
seem a little high when compared with Lewis–Faning's figures,
which were derived from direct questioning. However, Lewis–
Faning admits that his sample is likely to have under-represented birth controllers and that many women probably
declined to give their full histories. Nevertheless, the trend
that both report is unambiguous (see Table VIII, page 41).
Matras (1965b), Westoff *et al* (1954), Freedman, Whelpton
and Campbell (1959), Westoff, Potter, Sagi and Mishler (1961),
Westoff, Potter and Sagi (1963), Whelpton, Campbell and
Patterson (1966) and Rainwater (1965) all provide similar

---

[8]Further survey, subsequent to that reported by Rowntree and Pierce, carried
out by the Population Investigation Committee at the London School of Economics. A stratified random sample of 2200 women under 60 whose marriages had
remained intact to their 45th birthday were interviewed in 1967. The analysis,
which will include direct comparisons with the Rowntree and Pierce work, was
not available at the time of writing.

TABLE VIII

	Percentage of women reporting use of birth control at some point in marriage
*Birth cohort 1831–45**	19·5
Marriage cohort before 1910.	15
Marriage cohort 1910–19†	40
Marriage cohort 1920–24†	58
Marriage cohort 1925–29†	61
Marriage cohort 1930–34†	63
Marriage cohort 1935–39†	66
Marriage cohort 1930–39‡	65·5
Marriage cohort 1940–47†	55
Marriage cohort 1940–49‡	72·7
Marriage cohort 1950–59‡	70·1

Sources: *Matras (1965–66); †Lewis-Fanning (1949); ‡Rowntree and Pierce (1961–62). The latters' figure for the 1930s cohorts corresponds well with Lewis-Faning's. The discrepancy for the 1940s is accounted for by the fact that at the time of his survey, not all Lewis-Faning's couples in this cohort had reached the end of their family building, when contraceptive practice increases. A similar reason explains the low figure for the 1950s, which in later surveys will doubtless turn out to be higher.

information for the United States, although the historical data is less good there. Ninety-six per cent of the fecund white couples in the 1960 Growth of American Families study had used or expected to use some form of birth control during their marriage. It is clear, then, that—put at its very simplest— the proportion of couples practising some form of birth control has moved from under a quarter to practically all during the period of transition. It is likely that this pattern prevails in all presently advanced countries, whenever the period of transition began.

All the British and American studies agree in discerning three main trends in the practice of birth control, in addition to that of increasing absolute usage. First, birth control has always been more prevalent in the higher social classes or status groups, although the differentials have gradually narrowed. Secondly, birth control intensifies as the desired parity is approached, and is thus more intense later in the marriage. Half of the Growth of American Families sample in 1960 did not use contraception before the first birth. And thirdly, there has been a change in the relative distribution of the methods used. To begin with, *interruptus* and *reservatus* (usually classed together as 'withdrawal' in the literature) are the commonest methods. Forty-three per cent of the recently married couples in Lewis–Faning's sample in the late 1940s still used this method, and a survey in Grenoble in 1961–62 showed that two-thirds of those who had been using birth control relied mainly on it too (Siebert and Sutter, 1964). Withdrawal is overtaken by male and female appliances, from the douche through the condom to the diaphragm, and very recently oral contraceptives have begun to dominate the field, at least in the United States. The novelty of the last change is illustrated by Westoff and Ryder (1967). The contraceptive pill was not used by any couples sampled in 1960 or 1955, but by 1965 it had become the commonest method of control among the recently married.[9] It is likely that those countries, such as France, in which more traditional methods are the rule, will by-pass the stage of substantial reliance on appliances of the familiar kinds and instead adopt oral contraception and intra-uterine devices in the near future.

Good information on the effectiveness of birth control pre-dates the widespread introduction of the pill, and thus refers to the period in which *interruptus* and *reservatus*, together with various mechanical appliances (excluding I.U.D.s) were pre-

[9]As mentioned above, the results of the 1967 Population Investigation Committee survey, which includes questions on methods used, are not available at the time of writing. Sir Dugald Baird has also done some work one the use of the pill in Aberdeen and this will be published in *The Lancet*.

dominant. About 20 per cent of Lewis–Faning's later cohorts admitted to an unwanted child, while 88 per cent of the users in Rowntree and Pierce's sample said that they had been successful in limiting the size and controlling the timing of their births. This latter figure is suspiciously large, and has been challenged (Henry, 1962). The results from the analysis of the 1960 Growth of American Families study conform more to Lewis–Faning's, and are the most recent available for an advanced country. In that sample, 21 per cent of the couples planned all of their pregnancies by deliberately stopping contraception in order to conceive; 25 per cent began using contraception after one or two births, but stayed within their desired and expected size; 37 per cent had had one or more accidental or other unplanned conceptions but again had not exceeded their desires; and only 17 per cent had had one or more conceptions more than either the husband or the wife or both had originally wanted. Contraceptive effectiveness in several studies has been found to vary inversely with desired family size, and bearing in mind that expected family sizes are always slightly higher than desired ones (see above, II), the expectations of these four groups were 2·4, 2·8, 3·4 and 4·1 respectively. One point to emerge from this G.A.F. data is that while only 17 per cent reported that they had been unsuccessful in controlling their ultimate family *size*, fully 79 per cent had not controlled their timing or *spacing*. This difference becomes crucial when examining the social and economic factors lying behind differential birth control (see below). It is, of course, likely that the rates of contraceptive success amongst those couples using the pill will be found to be higher than these figures suggest, due rather to the technical infallibility of the method rather than to any significant increase in contraceptive knowledge over the period.[10]

(c) *In Developing Societies*
Simple inferences from the information that we have on the practice and effectiveness of birth control in industrial societies,

[10]Assessing contraceptive effectiveness is a complicated business; the traditional methods, derived from Pearl (1940), have been criticised by, among others, Potter, who has proposed a different method which he has used against data from the Princeton study (1966; 1967).

particularly from the facts that such control is less frequent and less effective in the lower social classes and that effectiveness in this sphere is inversely related to desired family size, quite apart from any other sociological knowledge we may have, leads one to expect that the practice and effectiveness of birth control in developing societies will be considerably behind the observed levels in industrial societies. 'In almost all studies that have been conducted, an overwhelming majority of respondents approve (of) the idea of family planning, a large majority express some interest in learning more about it, and in the developing countries very few have detailed information about birth control, since only small proportions use such methods' (Mauldin, 1965b). Proportions of those who have used them vary widely. Mauldin (1965a) has collected some figures to display the range: 1 per cent in rural Mysore; 6 per cent in urban Mysore; 3 per cent in Trivandrum; 3 to 8 per cent in villages near Delhi; 8 to 18 per cent in Lahore; 21 to 36 per cent in Dacca; 4 to 9 per cent in Korea; 24 per cent in Turkey; 1·5 per cent in rural Egypt; 12 per cent in semi-urban Egypt; and 17 per cent in urban Egypt. Not all developing areas, however, display these depressingly low figures. Miro (1966) has recently shown that the proportion of all women legally married or living in common-law consensual unions in Latin America and using some form of birth control varies, in the cities, from 37·5 per cent in Mexico City to 65 per cent in San José. Taking women with university education, of course, the proportion rises to between 62 and 78 per cent (with the curious exception of Mexico City again, at 50·9). Moreover, there is no significant difference between the rates for Catholics and non-Catholics. The island of Taiwan (Formosa), as least as much for political as for humane reasons, has received a great deal of American investment in the form of men, materials and money for birth control programmes since 1962, and by 1964, 34 per cent of the married women in the urban areas had used some form of contraception, but this is an exceptional figure for a substantially peasant society. There is, in any case, some evidence that Taiwan was moving towards the latter stages of the demographic transition of its own accord, and thus that the impressive decline in the birth rate there, from 50 in 1951 to

32·7 represents a force of social change to which the family planning programmes have found it relatively easy to adapt. Nevertheless, the birth rate, from declining at about 1·7 per cent per year between 1951 and 1963 to a faster drop of 4·4 per cent between 1964 and 1966, does seem to show some response to the control programmes. Moreover, the rate in the city of Taichung, the scene of an especially intensive campaign, has declined more rapidly than others in other cities. Davis (1967), though, is sceptical of the relationship between more rapid decline and the introduction of the birth control programmes, arguing that the period of more rapid deceleration since 1963 corresponds to the period from 1947 to 1955 in Japan, a natural fast period of decline that occurs late in every demographic transition. He also considers that the at first sight promising results from Taichung mean no more than that couples in that city responded with alacrity to cheap and available methods, but that they would have very soon controlled their fertility with the more expensive abortions that are traditional on the island. And there is force in his criticism that the present birth control programme there has no intention of persuading the inhabitants to alter their reproductive goals, as distinct from persuading them to realise them more effectively. The demography of Taiwan has been well documented in a series of thorough articles (Tauber, 1961; Freedman, Pen, Takeshita, and Sun, 1963; Freedman, Takeshita and Sun, 1964; Berelson and Freedman, 1964; Freedman, 1965; Takeshita, 1966; 1967; Collver, Speare and Liu, 1966–67).

Not only is the issue of birth control in the developing countries morally, economically, socially and thus politically the most burning one in modern population studies, but it is also the one in which the most rapid changes are taking place. For this reason I shall make no attempt here to make any further summaries of progress to date and prospects for the future. Recent discussions of such progress can be found in Berelson (1966), Bogue (1967), Kiser (1962), Sheps and Ridley (1965), Ohlin (1967), Muramatsu and Harper (1966) and Behrman (1969). The International Planned Parenthood Federation's *Newsletter* and conference reports and the Population Council's periodic *Studies in Family Planning*, as well as the academic journals, report on current projects and evaluations. The Indian experiments, in many ways both the most depressing and the most interesting, can be followed in the *Newsletter* of the Indian Demographic Research and Training Centre. In the United States, the population research institutes at the universities of Chicago, Michigan and California (Berkeley), together with departments of public health in universities such as Johns Hopkins are all involved with training, research and evaluation on birth control programmes abroad and frequently publish reports of their activities.

There is little reasonable doubt that the methods of birth control as described here are responsible for the majority of fertility control in the United States, Britain and Scandinavia. If the programmes to introduce the pill and especially the cheap and effective intra-uterine devices to women in developing societies succeed (and such programmes are not without their critics: see Stycos, 1962), it will be the case that such methods will also come to dominate there. However, it is at present fair to say that whenever couples in these societies want to control their fertility, they still overwhelmingly resort to other methods. These include sterilisation and induced foetal mortality (or abortion), although perhaps no longer, on any important scale, infanticide.[11]

4   STERILISATION

Surgical sterilisation seems to have been first proposed by one Dr. John Blundell in London in 1823, to avoid the necessity of repeated Caesarean sections or destruction of the infant in cases of severe pelvic contraction. I know of no evidence indicating its use before this, and it is unlikely, considering the medical knowledge of pre-industrial and primitive societies, that it would have been practised before the nineteenth century. The much easier methods of abortion and infanticide were available.

Male or female sterilisation as a method of contraception is of limited incidence, and apparently restricted to Puerto Rico, Japan and India, and to a much lesser extent, places like the United States and Britain. In no country does it appear

---

[11] I discuss Davis and Blake's tenth intermediate variable, involuntary foetal mortality, in the Appendix.

to have a significant effect when compared with other methods, and as less drastic contraceptive methods become medically and socially feasible, it inevitably declines. It has yet to reach its peak in India, where at most only two per thousand of the population (more males than females) have been operated upon. In Puerto Rico it has had perhaps its highest recorded instance, although the fact that it became legal for social reasons after 1937 has not removed the pattern of sterilisation prevailing in all societies from the island: most sterilisations are performed towards the end of the fecund period (Tietze, 1965a; 1965b; Hill, Stycos and Back, 1959). It is reported (Tauber and Oreleans, 1966; Tien, 1964–65) that sterilisation is acceptable and available in mainland China, but there is no reliable information on its extent and effect. Whether male sterilisation after the completion of family building in the West will increase remains to be seen.

5   ABORTION AND INFANTICIDE

'Foetal mortality from voluntary causes' includes essentially what is known as abortion, and there is considerable evidence of its use in all sorts of social organisations. Carr–Saunders (1922), Devereaux (1955), Ford (1954), Himes (1936) and Nag (1962) all report evidence of the use of abortion to regulate births in primitive societies, and all exept Devereaux also review the evidence for infanticide. Once again, however, we are at a loss to know how to assess this evidence. Firth (1936) on the one hand reports that abortion is occasionally used by unmarried girls in Tikopia to prevent a birth, but does not consider it to be at all common among married women. Levi-Strauss (1955) on the other hand is firm in stating that infanticide is common among the South American Nambik-wara, and is the only method used to regulate the population firmly to about replacement level. Between these extremes, the effect of such mortality is an open guess. It is more likely that regulation was effected by high infant, child and adult mortality rates in primitive societies, and that abortion and infanticide were only resorted to in exceptional circumstances. The widespread evidence of rituals designed to enhance fertility, and of numerous joyful songs celebrating births is contradictory to any belief that primitive populations felt it necessary to resort to induced foetal and infant mortality to any great extent, and as I have said above, there is little evidence that the majority of such societies practised any other form of fertility control. What is interesting is that these populations, with perhaps the single exception of the Tully River blacks (and just possibly Malinowski's Trobrianders), knew that interrupting coitus prevented insemination. The question is not so much did they know how to control births, but why did they choose not to do so?

In so far as any certainty is possible when assessing the frequency of contraceptive methods, it is certain that infanticide is no longer an important method of fertility control. Abortion, on the other hand, 'well may be the most widely used single method in the world today' (Freedman, 1966). This generalisation compounds what are probably the relatively low rates in Western countries with the startlingly high ones in others, including the transitional cases of Japan and European Europe. Between a quarter and half of all women reporting fertility control in Chile, for example (Romero, 1966) specify abortion as the method used. Since abortion for social reasons is not legal in Chile, and since respondents are usually reluctant to admit having induced them in these circumstances (Hill, Stycos and Back, 1959), these results are very credible. The combination of a progressive and informed elite, a Catholic culture and a large number of very fertile poor (among whom the birth rate exceeds forty) has produced great concern about what Romero calls the 'disaster' of illegal abortions in Chile, and the consequent research is good. Abortion tends to be more frequent among those who have already tried some other method of control, and of 46 per cent reporting abortions in Santiago, Concepción and Antafagasta, 75 per cent had experienced at least three. Curiously, resort to abortion was commonest among the most intensely Catholic.[12] Illegal abortion is also exceptionally prevalent in Korea and Taiwan.

The same cultural conditions, specifically the absence of the Christian moralities which place a higher value on life than on a satisfactory life, made abortion acceptable to the Japanese

---

[12]No doubt a spurious correlation with poverty, high fertility and despair. However, Catholicism has very little effect on birth control attitudes and practices in Latin America: see Chapter V.

when threatened with what they saw as overpopulation in the post-war years (Muramatsu, 1966). The Eugenic Protection Law of 1948 allows the interruption of a pregnancy in a woman 'whose health may be affected seriously from the physical or economic viewpoint by the continuation of pregnancy or by confinement', (Tietze, 1965a; Muramatsu, 1960; Tauber, 1958). The largest abortion rate was recorded in 1955, and by 1963 it had dropped slightly, although still in the ratio of 60: 100 to live births. Registration is said to be only 50 to 70 per cent complete. With such an effective birth control policy (and it will be remembered that the Japanese also exhibit a variety of other demographic responses to rising population), it is not surprising that at age 40–44 the Japanese have the lowest proportion of never-married women of almost any society.

Abortions are freely available in Eastern Europe,[13] and range from 23 per 100 live births (1962) in Poland to 140 (1964) in Hungary (Tietze, 1964; 1965a; 1965b; Klinger, 1966). The Hungarian birth rate, at the very low level of 13·0 in 1964, has declined by over 40 per cent since the early 1950s and Tietze attributes this decline largely to the abortion programme (1964). It is also notable that the two European societies outside the Soviet bloc with very low birth rates, Iceland and Greece (Valaoras *et al*, 1964–65), are also ones in which abortions are easily obtainable. In Iceland, however, rapid progress is being made with the promotion of techniques to prevent conception, and it is likely that the situation there will come to resemble that in the other Scandinavian countries, in which although there are liberal abortion programmes, other methods of fertility control are also well developed and widely practiced (Myrdal, 1941; Tietze, 1965a).

The extent of resort to abortion in less liberal societies, such as Britain, France and the United States, is very much disputed. The extent of the dispute can be gauged from an estimate for illegal abortions in the United States that can be no more precise than suggesting that the true figure lies between 200,000 and 1,200,000 (Calderone, 1958). The con-

[13]The U.S.S.R., the German Democratic Republic, Poland, Hungary, Czechoslovakia, Hungary, Bulgaria, Rumania (until recently), Yugoslavia but not Albania.

tribution of the after-effects of abortion to maternal deaths in the United States is increasing, and suggests that abortion may be increasing there. Ryder and Westoff (1967), examining the methods of fertility control in the States in 1955, 1960 and 1965 find an increase in the resort to 'other methods' over that period. If the figure is nearer 1,200,000, illegal abortions are one third of live births. A similar picture has been found in Britain and France (Family Planning Association, 1966; Weill–Hallé, 1967).

The Taiwan, Japanese and Chilean evidence, together with that for Britain, France and the United States, in which it seems certain that the resort to abortion is more frequent among women already using some other form of fertility control and more frequent at parities of three and four (like other methods), suggests a pattern in which the termination of pregnancies increases with the desire to control fertility, but that as the availability of easier methods increases, so abortion declines. Sweden and Denmark appear to be at the end of this stage in the transition, Chile and other countries nearer the beginning. The point is most clearly made by the East European countries, where the pressure to control fertility is high, abortion legal and easily available, and thus frequent. It does not seem likely that a society will choose abortion in preference to other methods if those methods are available and reliable (Mehlan, 1966).

6 SUMMARY

For modern populations, the answer to the first of the two questions that I stated at the beginning of the chapter is fairly straightforward, and simple and generally valid: in these populations, women expose themselves to the risk of conception through regular cohabitation with men for the great majority of their fecund lives, and certainly for nearly all of the most fecund period (20–24). To the second question, however, the answers are less clear. Traditionally, *coitus interruptus* and *reservatus* together with abortion have been used to restrict fertility, and more at the end than at the beginning of the marriage. This pattern still prevails in most developing countries and in pockets of backwardness and poverty in industrial societies. More recently, various contraceptive devices, at first male and later female ones, have replaced these two in industrial societies. Most recently, oral contraceptives and, to a much lesser extent, intra-uterine devices have been adopted by these populations. Most developing societies to which modern methods of birth control have been introduced have by-passed this stage, and where they use such methods they are characteristically I.U.D.s and, less often, oral contraceptives. With the doubtful exceptions of countries such as Japan, Taiwan and Korea (and perhaps China), the effects of these new programmes are still to reveal themselves.

In apparent contradiction to the way in which I have reviewed the literature on the variables intervening between social norms and observed fertility, it is perhaps worth concluding by emphasising the counsel of analytic perfection that Davis and Blake offer:

> One cannot say, as is frequently implied in the literature, that some of these variables are affecting fertility in one society but not in another. *All* of the variables are present in *every* society. This is because . . . each one *is* a variable— it can operate either to reduce or to enhance fertility . . . In other words, the absence of a specific practice does not imply 'no influence' on fertility, because this very absence is a form of influence. It follows that the position of any society, if stated at all, must be stated on all eleven variables.

CHAPTER IV

Explaining Fertility

At the beginning of the last chapter, I said that the study of the social determinants of fertility does not entirely escape the disputes that rage elsewhere in sociology over the proper strategies of enquiry. It is only immune in so far as there is not and indeed cannot be much argument over the relevant intervening variables; they are logically entailed in the nature of the demographic system (Ryder, 1963–64). But once embarked on an explanation of the determinants of the dependent and the intervening variables together, one is propelled into the methodological cross-fire so familiar in sociology.

I THE PROBLEM OF CAUSALITY

In the rest of my argument, I shall assume that we are looking both for causal explanations and for satisfactory predictions. The second of these, of course, presents fewer problems than the first. For predictions we simply need law-like generalisations that can serve as premises in a syllogism, such that once we know 'if A then B' and once we have 'A' we can predict 'B'. These generalisations can be between any two phenomena, and they can be either deterministic or probabilistic. Causal explanations, however, are more demanding. The necessary condition for being able to talk of a causal statement was formulated by Hume: 'we may define a cause to be an object, followed by another, and where all the objects similar to the first are followed by objects similar to the second'. That, however, could equally describe a deterministic law-like generalisation. For my purposes, I shall take such a generalisation to be synomymous with a causal statement.

The problem of explaining human behaviour, however, does not disappear once these elementary distinctions have been made and the conditions for causal statements clarified.

We must still ask what sorts of factors are acceptable as causes of that behaviour. As I hope to show in the following argument, it seems to me that in taking the analytically easier course, sociologists looking at fertility (and, by implication, at many other phenomena) have, deliberately or not, avoided facing this question. This is understandable, since to do so is almost inevitably to illuminate the deficiencies of the analytical method that they adopt.

This method is surely familiar. It has been formalised for sociologists by the Columbia School, in particular in the work of Lazarsfeld and his students, and when sociologists talk of 'methodology' it is this that they usually have in mind. In so far as practitioners of this approach, which can simply if somewhat crudely be called 'statistical empiricism', deal with causality they do so in strictly Humean terms. That is, they take causality to be nothing more than the constant conjunction of two discrete objects in a determinate order over time. In so doing, they commit themselves to the principle that the two (or more) phenomena that they are trying to relate must be quite distinct: were they not so, any propositions linking them would tend towards the tautologous. This may seem a trivial and obvious point to emphasise, but as I hope to show presently, it has been erroneously, and strenuously, invoked to challenge the kind of explanation that I wish to propose. Statistical empiricists, as well as subscribing to the constant conjunction definition of causality and to the principle that causally-related objects must be absolutely discrete, tend also to adhere to the stringent empiricist canons of observation. In practice, of course, few if any adhere completely to the kind of position advocated by men like Eddington, who would have nothing of concepts like 'heat' and 'force' and preferred to discuss physics in terms of connections between observations of meter-readings. Most empiricists (and thus most scientists) allow themselves a certain latitude of speculation, a certain amount of what might more precisely be called 'ontological imagination' in their work.[1]

There are, then, two principles in the empiricist canon which are logically related, those of constant conjunction and

[1]Harré (1961) provides an excellent, concise discussion of this and other issues in the logic and testing of theories.

discrete objects, and a further one which tends, contingently, to go with them, that of the restriction of the discussion to the directly observable. This latter contingent tendency has its roots in the history of scientific practice and I will assume that it is obvious and familiar enough to remain relatively un-elaborated at this point. Consider, now, what the implications of these three are for explanations of fertility.

Suppose there to be a perfect correlation between working mothers and low fertility (as I point out in Chapter V, there is a very good, although by no means perfect one). Suppose further (which is definitely not the case) that it is clear that the correlation is such that low fertility is always consequent upon mothers working. The three principles would all seem to be met: there is a constant conjunction in a determinate order in time, the objects are discrete, and both can be observed directly without the need for persuasive conceptualisation or indirect indicators. A statistical empiricist would thus be quite consistent with his beliefs in referring to the causal effect of working mothers on low fertility. At first sight, there is nothing wrong with this. Were it true, it would be precisely one of those informative causal generalisations that sociologists have long been encouraging each other to produce.

However, although it may be a perfectly satisfactory causal statement from a logical point of view it is, I think, informa-tively unsatisfying. When we say that working mothers *cause* low fertility we can only make the statement intelligible to ourselves by hypothesising an intervening mechanism. It is almost certain that this mechanism will refer to the mental states of the women, to their appraisal of the feelings about their roles and to the decisions that they have taken on the basis of those appraisals and feelings. Only then, when we have said that working women cause low fertility *because* they cannot afford resources for a job and a larger family (or something of that sort) do we feel that we have properly explained their behaviour.

But it is not only common sense that inclines us to believe that the mental states of actors must be invoked in an explana-tion (whether causal or not) of their behaviour. There is also a very good argument that this must be the case. This argu-ment starts from the question of what it is to identify a piece of behaviour in the first place. At its very simplest, it goes like this. A man may raise his arm, and we can fairly unequivocally describe that movement in behavioural terms. But it is not clear that we have understood what he is doing. He may be saluting, greeting someone, waving good-bye, stretching, asking to be able to put a question and so forth. There are many possibilities, and we can only decide between them by understanding his own description of it. This will identify it for us. Now, it can be argued (e.g. Winch, 1958) that what we use to identify the behaviour as a particular action are the actor's intentions; to the question 'what are you doing in raising your arm?' we want a reply of the kind 'I am asking to be able to put a question', and that reply is also his intention in raising his arm. If that is the case, then intentions, reasons and so forth are logically related to our description of the action. The connection between the two, the intention and the action, is an internal, logical one; and if it is of such a kind, then it cannot possibly be a causal relationship, since one of the criteria for two objects being in a potentially causal relationship is that they shall be discrete and contingently related. We cannot explain something with the concept we have already used to describe it. Therefore, reasons, intentions and so on cannot be causes. The kind of explanation that they provide is of another kind, and it is logically mistaken to assimilate that to causal explanations. Given that mental states are extremely difficult to observe with any known validity and reliability, and that they are questionably distinct from the actions of which they are supposed to be causes (as the argument in the last paragraph would want them to be), it is not surprising that those of an empiricist cast of mind have tended to keep well away from them. This is what I meant when I said earlier that in taking an analytically easy course many sociologists avoid facing the central issue in explaining action.

However, the contention that the relationship between reasons and actions is an internal, logical one and not an external, contingent one has its challengers, and I am inclined to accept the latters' case. It is simple, and rests upon the point that it is possible to conceive both of a reason without a consequent action and of an action made for several reasons. Given this possibility, there cannot be a one-to-one logical relationship between the two, but there must on the contrary be an empirically problematic contingent one (even allowing for the fact that an action cannot occur without a reason, or it would not be an action, and that that reason enables us to define the action). Reasons can, after all, be causes (Davidson, 1963; MacIntyre, 1967).

But, it is retorted, even if they can be, they are not. This is because they do not constitute general causal statements, and it is agreed that in some sense causal laws must also be general laws (Hart and Honoré, 1959). It is suggested that in fact we can get generalisations about connections between reasons and actions, but as Davidson says 'the suggestion is delusive . . . because generalisations connecting reasons and actions are not—and cannot be sharpened into—the kind of law on the basis of which accurate predictions can reliably be made. If we reflect on the way in which reasons determine choice, decision and behaviour', he continues, 'it is easy to see why this is so. What emerges, in the *ex post facto* atmosphere of explanation and justification, as *the* reason frequently was, to the agent at the time of action one consideration among many, *a* reason. Any serious theory for predicting action on the basis of reasons must find a way of evaluating the relative force of various desires and beliefs in the matrix of decision; it cannot take as its starting point the refinement of what is to be expected from a single desire'. Davidson concludes by saying that the practical syllogism, which does for most predictive statements, will not do for a predictive science of action.

Davidson himself, however, offers a solution to the dilemma which I find plausible. If, on the one hand, Hume meant that a singular causal statement of the form 'A caused B' must imply a general causal statement linking the predicates of 'A' and 'B', then the Hart and Honoré objection stands. If, on the other hand, Hume only meant that a singular causal statement of the form 'A caused B' must imply a general causal statement linking true descriptions of 'A' and 'B', then it is possible to talk of A causing B when either or both of the objects 'A' and 'B' occurred on only that one occasion. The singular is also the general, and the difficulty is circumvented. This solution depends, of course, upon a weak and contentious interpretation of Hume. For my purposes, however, it will serve. [2]

I have now provided a general answer to my earlier question about what sorts of factors are acceptable as causes of behaviour. Before going on with a specification of the kinds of reasons that might be useful in explanations of fertility, I want to deal briefly with a possible sociological objection to what I have already said. This would be to the effect that in insisting that individual mental states must be invoked in explanations of behaviour I am covertly subscribing to the reviled canons of so-called 'psychological reductionism'. To see psychological reductionism as an error (and I use the description merely because it has some currency among sociologists) rests in turn upon an erroneous understanding of what is involved in providing a sociological explanation. As I said in Chapter I, sociologists are those behavioural scientists charged with normative explanations of behaviour. A little thought will immediately reveal that an explanation in terms of norms necessarily requires a reference to the mental states of the actors: where else do norms exist, and where else can I observe them? To remove norms from the individuals who express them is to plunge into the metaphysical jungle that ensnares those sociologists who talk of individuals and of norms, and of the internalisation of norms, with little thought for exactly how the norms are to be grasped empirically. My argument throughout this chapter implies that explanations of behaviour must begin with individuals, whatever theoretical constructs one may wish to build subsequently.

2 A CAUSAL MODEL

Now, what sorts of reasons are candidates as causes of fertility? Ironically, given what I have said so far about the confusions of sociological explanation, the sociology of fertility is comparatively well supplied with explanations of the kind that I have been advocating, and the irony derives from the fact that much of the work in the field has been done by economists. Economists, of course, begin from propositions or axioms about dispositions, motives, reasons and so on in

[2]A useful essay and collecton of papers on the arguments of the last four paragraphs can be found in White (1968).

their explanatory models. Hence the presence of such factors in some existing explanatory accounts of fertility.

Classically, economics rested on the assumption that individuals maximised utility. Utility, it was felt, represented some psychological quantity, like pleasure or pain. This is not a testable proposition. Only when particular utilities, such as income, leisure time or status are specified does it become empirically interesting and potentially refutable. It has often been assumed that the general utilitarian model also assumed that individuals were rational. Whatever economists may have assumed or still do assume in their models, however, this does not follow necessarily from the first assumption. If I say that individuals maximise utility and leave it at that, without specifying what the particular utilities might be, I cannot be refuted from evidence. But if I say that they are rational in the sense of consumer's rationality used by economists, in that they will always prefer more rather than less of a good, other things being equal, then I am on the contrary open to such refutation. I also open myself to it when I assert that individuals are rational in the Weberian sense, that they logically relate means to ends. This is a sense of rationality distinct from the previous one. It is important for the rest of my argument that these three notions, the maximisation of utility, consumer rationality and Weberian *Zweckrationalität*, should be kept distinct. In choosing to follow a particular version of the utility model, I am not prejudging the issue of whether or not couples are always rational in their fertility behaviour. In an area in which irrationality and nonrationality are so conspicuous, that would be foolish. [3]

It has been frequently pointed out (e.g. Barry, 1965) that the notion of utility is both dangerous and unnecessary in such models: dangerous in that it implies an underlying and thus unverifiable psychological quantity, and unnecessary in that one can, given a set of stated preferences by the actor or actors, explain their behaviour in terms of the reasoning used to realise these preferences in the prevailing constraints imposed by the supply of resources. I certainly take the first point.

[3]The use of models of this kind in sociology is rare, but prominent. In addition to the most familiar Homans, there is the work of Blau (1964) and Simon (1967). I return to the more general implications in Chapter VI.

Those few attempts that have been made to suggest what the 'underlying' utility of children might be (such as Wyatt's ingenious but pretty far-fetched Freudian notion (1967) that children resolve the woman's problem of inner duality) are not especially helpful. The second point would seem to be largely terminological, once one is clear that no reference is being made to underlying psychological dispositions or whatever in the use of the notion of 'utility'. I shall therefore continue to use this concept, and postpone a more thorough general examination of the sociological implications and, dare I say it, utility of the model until Chapter VI.

Early discussions of the application of this sort of model to fertility assumed that there was an indifference curve for children just as there would be for cars or paintings, leaving aside the problems of decreasing marginal utility (Becker, 1960). Becker thus inferred that as income rises so fertility will rise too, since more children can be supplied. He pointed out that, once the inverse relation between income and contraceptive knowledge and effectiveness was removed, there was a positive association between income and fertility, and that this proved his point.

Duesenberry (1960) contested Becker's assumption that parents are free to choose how much they spend on children. Becker argues, in essence, that parents are free to substitute other goods for expenditure on their children: they can, in his terms, have high quality or low quality children, quality being indicated by the amount spent on them. Duesenberry argues that this freedom is illusory. A middle class couple does not in fact have the choice of spending enough on four children to enable them to finish high school and no more, or to spend enough on them to enable them to graduate from a college or university, and thus the choice to substitute another good, such as a second car, in the first case. They are circumscribed by the social conventions of their reference groups. Duesenberry puts it well: 'Economics is all about how people make choices. Sociology is all about why they don't have any choices to make'. It would be as false to assume that this hypothetical couple are totally constrained in any crude sociologically deterministic sense as to assume that they are completely free to dispose of their income as they wish.

5

Easterlin (1969) has developed this argument between Becker and Duesenberry. What Duesenberry is talking about, Easterlin rightly contends, are norms; and norms are conceptually equivalent to tastes in the economists' language.[4] It would thus seem that sociologists and economists could fruitfully get together, the former making use of the kind of model that economists use to describe and predict consumption, and the latter paying more attention to the variable in their model that they most often neglect: namely, tastes.

3   THE MODEL APPLIED

There are four studies of fertility which support my argument here. One is based on secondary material from primitive societies (Douglas, 1966); a second on similar material from a contemporary situation (Easterlin, 1962; 1966); and the other two on direct information about the actor's reasoning (Banks, 1954; Rainwater, 1960; Rainwater, 1965). Many other studies include more incidental data on reasons, but none makes them central to the proposed explanations.

Douglas considers four primitive groups, the Pelly Bay Eskimos, the Rendille, the Tikopians and—less obviously primitive—the Nambudiri Brahmins, and argues that their attempts to control fertility can all be seen in the context of a 'concern for scarce social resources': that is, a desire to maximise some particular utility or set of utilities. The Netsilik Eskimos of the Pelly Bay area regularly kill off a proportion of their female babies. This dwindling people is pitted against an exceptionally harsh environment, and it has been argued that the female infanticide (recorded in 1923 as 38 deaths out of 96 births from 18 marriages) serves to balance the sex ratio in adulthood, by which time there has been a heavy male mortality. The heavy cost, noted by one observer, of severe competition for women was not considered by him to outweigh the benefit to the group's survival that came from the infanticides. As Douglas points out, this sort of example, in which population regulation is practised to ensure simple survival, the basic utility, is rare. More common are the sorts of reasons given by the other three groups.

[4] I discuss the validity of this equation in Chapter VI.

The Rendille, in Kenya, have an economy based on camel herds. The Rendille believe camel stocks to be fixed (the reproduction rate of these beasts is evidently low), and, through emigration, monogamy, a late age of marriage for women and the ritual murder of boys born on Wednesdays or after the circumcision of the eldest brother, they regulate their own rate of increase. At first sight, this too would seem to be an example of that situation in which population is regulated for sheer survival. However, the camel herds, being the staple scarce resource, are also the economic foundation of the stratification system and the symbolic order of Rendille society. Any disruption in the pattern of allocation and transfer that has been evolved would threaten this structure and thus threaten the very foundations of the tribe. The Rendille can thus be seen to be also controlling population in the service of maximising the utility of social order.

I have already discussed the demography of the Tikopia in Chapter III. The reasons that they have for controlling their population through intermittent contraception, abortion, infanticide and emigration have been excellently documented by Firth, and Douglas repeats these. Firth noticed that in conditions of famine the number of deaths by starvation on the island was negligible, yet it was under such conditions that population was most severely controlled. The Tikopians explained that the supply of ceremonial foods, such as coconut cream, fell during famines. Without such foods, they could not have feasts. (Without feasts, of course, although this would not be part of their own explanation, they could not give ritual expression to the structure of their society, and without such expression there would be severe sociological costs.) Shaming most Western societies, and paying tribute by example to Rousseau's conception of democracy in small societies, the Tikopians met during periods of difficulty and discussed their immediate population policy.

A similar utility is valued by the Nambudiri Brahmins, a rich and exclusive land-owning caste in Southern India. Fertility is controlled by the device of only allowing the eldest sons to marry which, by cutting down the number of marriages and thus the number of fertile women, restricts births. The other sons may seek release with women of lower castes, but the daughters, if they do not manage to obtain a husband from within the Nambudiri, are condemned to permanent celibacy and spinsterhood. The utility in this case is the continuing hegemony of the caste, a hegemony that is dependent upon the continuing stability of their lands.

Easterlin's work has been on fairly long-term variations in fertility: specifically, the fluctuations in the timing of births to post-war cohorts in the United States. His thesis is simple but cogent. The baby boom of the early post-war period (leaving aside the temporary rise attributable to the delayed effects of the war itself) is, he suggests, a function of newly-married cohorts having a higher potential income (see Friedman, 1957) in a period of relatively low consumer preferences for material goods. The former is explained by an increased demand for labour in the United States economy, the latter by the fact that these people were socialised—and thus their preferences formed—in a period of comparatively stringent economic austerity. The subsequent decline in age-specific fertility in more recently married cohorts Easterlin attributes to the reverse causes. 'In recent years [he is writing in 1966] young persons' incomes have grown only hesitantly, and their unemployment rates have risen . . . [their] net worth position has declined, suggesting heavier pressure of liabilities . . . Finally, the young cohorts of recent years have come from wealthier backgrounds than their predecessors in the 1940s, and in all likelihood are entering the childbearing ages with the more expensive tastes for consumer goods thereby acquired'. In short, relative incomes are down and preferences are up: the net effect is a reduction in fertility. Easterlin is cautious in attributing all the variance in fertility trends since the war to these causes (it is obvious, for example, that contraceptive efficiency has been increasing), but it nevertheless seems eminently plausible. Above all, from the point of view of this chapter, it stands as an explanation, presenting causal mechanisms. The doubtful elements in his discussion, for example his belief that an increased participation of women in the labour force indicates pressures on household incomes, while empirically questionable, do not challenge his model. If it were found, for example, that more people in more groups had adopted the norm that women should seek fulfilment outside the home, this would be one more preference to be set off against fertility (although, of course, odd in that it would be a preference that *raised* income).

Banks's account of the mechanisms lying behind the adoption of more restrictive family planning among the English middle classes in the 1870s is theoretically very similar. Banks, using as far as he is able contemporary documentary sources, assumes that preferences remained constant through the period of transition, and particularly that the preference for the prestige accruing to middle-class status was undiminished. As the decade proceeded, however, the costs of maintaining this status rose. There was an economic depression, the North-cote–Trevelyan reforms made it essential that candidates for the prized middle-class careers in the Civil Service were well-educated, and so forth. In Becker's terms, these parents were forced to have higher-quality children precisely at the time when the potential disposable income was falling. The net effect was a decline in fertility. Banks concludes by arguing that this syndrome diffused down through the social classes, and this separate argument is, as it is stated (and as I have argued above), misleading—if not actually false. Populations have been able to control fertility in times of adversity for millenia, and it will not do to suggest that the British working class did not control its fertility because of a lack of contraceptive knowledge. Further, this thesis rests on the assumption that they wished to, that the balance of utilities and costs was such as to induce a desire for fewer children. This is an as yet unanswered empirical question.[5] And suggestions such as that implied by Beshers (1967), that a Weberian *Zweckrationalität* had not yet diffused to this group remain at best as implausible and unproven hypotheses (but, it must be added, hypotheses of the right kind).

Rainwater's two studies, one of a sample of white working-class couples in Chicago and Cincinnati (1960), the other of a sample of middle- and working-class whites and working-class Negroes from these two cities, and, in addition, Oklahoma City (1965), are sociologically the most informative in the literature. There is more strictly demographic information,

[5]Banks (1954) should be read critically; his ingenuity frequently outruns his evidence, but this does not detract from the point I am making here.

of both dependent and intervening variables, in many other studies: for the United States, particularly in the Growth of American Families and Princeton work and in Kiser, Grabill and Campbell (1968). But essentially, Rainwater's sociological contribution lies in both documenting the rationale behind fertility behaviour and in also ferreting out those social and psychological forces that deflect the effective implementation of the decisions reached by such ratiocination. Rainwater is not explicit about his causal model: at one point, he refers to 'the culture and social system within each class subgroup which differentially influences behaviour', thus betraying a rather primitive understanding of sociological explanation. Nevertheless, he is clearly a sensitive and skilled observer, and this, together with his confessed disappointment with the more orthodox statistical surveys, leads him to provide virtually all the information that we need to give our model flesh.

He discusses rationales for family size in his book, *Family Design*. The commonest norm about family size was that 'one should not have more children than one can support, but one should have as many as one can afford'. He adds that 'affording a given size of family is . . . only superficially conceptualised as an economic matter'. The utilities desired by these couples were a maintained standard of living ('as many as one can afford'), psychic stability for themselves, a meaningful extra-domestic role for the wife (by some), psychic satisfactions for the children and a feeling of being morally responsible and not selfish. The first three lead to lower fertility; the last two to higher fertility. Unfortunately, Rainwater does not examine the strictly economic calculations, but his elaboration and documentation of the non-economic utilities is extremely useful. Described too in great detail, particularly in *And the Poor Get Children*, are the social preconditions for the mental states that lead to ineffective contraception. In sum, Rainwater's thesis that it is segregated conjugal role relationships characterised by poor communication, relatively deficient sexual relationships and so forth that induce poor contraception. In many working-class couples, these pressures are so strong as to obliterate any fully conscious rationales at all. Nevertheless, as has been argued elsewhere (Pohlman, 1965), and as Rainwater's research illustrates by example, wants (or desired utilities) can be *inferred* from skilled, extended interviewing.

In all these examples, from the Arctic, sub-tropical Africa, Polynesia, southern India, Victorian middle-class England and the contemporary United States, fertility behaviour, or associated methods of population regulation, can be understood and causally explained with a utility model. The utility model alone, being axiomatic, is also of course vacuous. However, as I suggested in the Introduction, the demand for a theory which is both general (as the utility model is, by definition) and non-trivial can be met by specifying the particular utilities that particular groups value, and the costs as they see them involved in realising these utilities.

4 SOME PROBLEMS

There is, lastly, one cloud over the promise of a utility model. This is that utilities are extremely difficult to measure. Not only do economists have difficulty in ranking, let alone applying interval or ratio scales to, purely economic preferences, but it is not even clear that one can assume equal preference intervals between successive quantities of a good. Indifference curve models are a device to avoid the direct and knotty problem of measuring utilities, but they can only do so by making certain assumptions about the ranking of preferences. It is reported that 'when one examines the way couples talk about the different sizes of families, one becomes aware that psychologically this is not a continuous distribution but a highly discontinuous one' (Rainwater, 1965). A re-analysis cf fertility preferences gained from interviews in the 1962 Detroit Area Study in terms of Coombs' ordered metric scale derived from what Coombs calls 'unfolding analysis' showed that the distance in the preference between two and four children represented less than 20 per cent of the distance between zero and six (Goldberg and Coombs, 1963). An interval scale would, of course, have predicted 33·3 per cent.

Moreover, inter-utility comparisons are even more difficult. Propositions of the form 'couple X prefers utility u to n extra children', essential to the kind of model that I have proposed, are hard to substantiate empirically. Economists have long faced the same problem when attempting to aggregate discrete consumption functions and determine substitutabilities (Friedman, 1957).

Nevertheless, this cannot be sufficient cause for abandoning the utility approach. As long as there is no exaggerated confidence about measurement (as in Hauser's (1962) 'it is assumed that satisfactory metrics can be found for the dependent and independent variables'), it should be possible to make a little progress. But it should be remembered that the statistical measures of association available for ordinally-scaled variables are still, unfortunately, very primitive and unreliable.

CHAPTER V

Social Correlates and Determinants

1 A CAUTIONARY TALE

The methodological implication of what I have been saying about explanations of fertility is simple. It is, to adapt Allport, that 'if you want to know why people do what they do, why not first ask them?' Since human fertility is not entirely determined by social factors of which the actors are aware, this will of course not provide all the answers. But its usefulness can be illustrated by a cautionary tale from the literature, which is an object lesson to the conventional practice of taking a number of variables—none of which refer to the actors' own explanations—and seeing where the best correlations lie. The tale is thus an example of the pitfalls of routine survey analysis as the Columbia School and others have long described it, and serves to warn one against too easy an acceptance of the many correlations between social factors and fertility that the literature reports, and which I devote most of this chapter to reviewing.

Stycos (1962–63) and Heer (1964–65) had both noticed a positive relation between fertility and economic development in parts of Latin America. Stycos' work was on Peru, and Heer's on Ecuador and Bolivia. Stycos suggested that the explanation might be that the greater marital instability of the economically less-advanced Indians, as compared with the Spanish-speaking population, led to a smaller exposure to the risk of conception. Heer cast doubt on this hypothesis, and suggested instead that the difference may be due to voluntary causes, such as abortion or infanticide. James (1966–67) re-examined their data, prompted it seems, by Stycos' tabulation of fertility in Peruvian *provincias* by altitude and the proportion of the population speaking Spanish. Stycos's results were as shown in Table X:

TABLE X

	Less than half Spanish-speaking	Half or more Spanish-speaking
Under 200m. ..	94*	96
200m. or higher ..	86	92

*refers to the mean child-woman ratio in each province; *Source:* Stycos, (1962–63).

The only association significant at the 0·05 level was that between the two means for the high *provincias*.[1] He thus concluded that ethnic status, as indicated by language, was a more powerful determinant of fertility than altitude. James suggests that Stycos' results would have been rather different had he dichotomised a little nearer the medians of the variables, and proceeds to test his suspicion against data for the larger administrative units of Peru and Bolivia, and for *provincias* in Ecuador. He finds that the product-moment correlations between fertility and altitude for Peru, Eucador and Bolivia are —0·805, —0·761 and —0·726 respectively. The relationship between fertility and altitude, holding language constant, is stronger than that between fertility and language, holding altitude constant. The conclusion therefore seems to be that altitude is more closely related to fertility than is economic development (if the indicators of the latter are accepted). Heer (1967) accepted James' recalculations.

These recalculations have themselves now been challenged. For reasons outside their control, the official birth registrations being so deficient, James and Heer used the ratio of children under five to women between 15 and 49 as their measure of fertility. Whitehead (1968) has taken up James' admission that such a statistic disguises the effect of infant mortality, and has presented scattered field evidence to show that such mortality is in fact very high in the high-altitude regions of Bolivia and Ecuador (and by implication, Peru). True crude brith rates may be as high as fifty, well in excess of those at lower altitudes. It is therefore unlikely that there can be any

[1]It is, in fact, not clear that Stycos's sample meets the requirements for the use of significance tests; this does not, however, affect the argument here.

significant effect of altitude on fecundity, either through the male or the female. What records there are do suggest, as James expected, that there are a large number of abortions; but these appear to be voluntary and not spontaneous and thus to have a social cause. Neither is there any suggestion that the high infant mortality is a direct product of living at high altitudes. Rather, it is explicable in terms of the social conditions of the depressed populations at these heights, populations that have yet to enjoy the substantial measures of preventive public health now enjoyed by the majority of developing communities. The most recent contribution to this debate at the time of writing (Bradshaw, 1969) confirms the tendency suggested by Whitehead from Peruvian data. Bradshaw considers that the under-registration in Indian Peru may have disguised a fertility in excess of that in the Spanish-speaking districts, and therefore that the fertility differentials in Peru are much more consistent with the pattern to be expected from the transition model than was at first thought.

This fascinating exchange of data and arguments contains three lessons. First, and most obviously, the greatest care has to be exercised in using deficient demographic data. The less refined such data are, the more likely are they to contain hidden effects that can make nonsense of one's inferences. Secondly, it reveals the dangers of simply taking hypotheses that fit one's preconceptions as a sociologist or biologist, and not testing for factors conventionally treated by other workers. And thirdly, it reveals how much more easily field evidence, including the direct interviewing of the childbearing population to elucidate their intentions as well as their fertility behaviour, can lead to more accurate causal imputations.

2 CORRELATES OF THE DEMOGRAPHIC TRANSITION

(a) *In General*

There is, however, little doubt that sociological, including economic, factors are mainly responsible for the so-called demographic transition in fertility and mortality over the past two hundred years. The problem is not that of mistaking a non-sociological process for a sociological one, but rather that of deciding which sociological factors have been responsible for which rate-changes (as well as deciding which rates changed in what directions and to what extent: see Chapter III). Sorting out the various factors requires a supply of information and a methodological sophistication that have only recently become realistic possiblities. The United Nations' review of the debate about the fertility transition (1953) illustrates how recently the leading authorities in the field were still somewhat at a loss to assess the relative contributions of the various factors, and the extent to which they were forced to resort to speculation. And so long as the relative contribution of various determinants is unknown, so it is impossible to begin to suggest a mechanism that can account for the change.

Ryder (1959) makes this plain when, in summarising the societal types that have accompanied the three main stages of the demographic transition, he points out that such a mechanism would necessarily be part of a wider explanatory theory of modernisation or development; and that we have no such theory. His summary nevertheless contains at least some of the building blocks for one. The first societal type is typified by high fertility and mortality, labour intensive agriculture, and consanguineal familism. In these societies, fertility is controlled by various combinations of infanticide, abortion and abstinence. Some peasant societies in the Far East still display these characteristics. Second is the type characterised by somewhat lower fertility and mortality, agriculture which is still labour intensive, but in which consanguineal familism has been replaced by a conjugal pattern and where fertility is controlled primarily by a later age at marriage. Such was pre-industrial Europe from the sixteenth century or so. Third and last is that type characteristic of the modern West, where fertility and mortality are low, industry replaces agriculture as the dominant economic activity, individualism predominates over familial values and in which fertility is mainly regulated by contraception within marriage.

There are two steps toward generating a more satisfactory account of the causal mechanism or mechanisms behind the transition. The first, to which I shall turn in a moment and on which most work has been done, is that of carefully distingushing which factors in which combinations followed each other with what rapidity in what societies. The second, consistent with what I have already argued in the previous two chapters, is that of providing an account of the changing rationales of prospective and actual parents under changing social conditions. These are complementary and both consequent upon accurately describing the specific demographic changes that have taken place (see Chapter III).

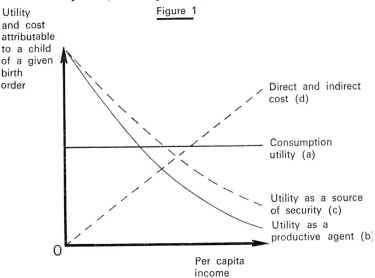

Figure 1

Utility and cost attributable to a child of a given birth order

Direct and indirect cost (d)

Consumption utility (a)

Utility as a source of security (c)

Utility as a productive agent (b)

Per capita income

Source: Leibenstein (1957 : 163).

Leibenstein (1957) has provided a speculative account of the changing utilities of children through the period of development which, although not completely tested, nevertheless exemplifies the kind of account that my previous arguments demand. It is illustrated in Figure I. He begins by assuming that the desire for children for their own sake remains constant over the period of rising per capita income (a), it also being a basic assumption of the whole theory that this income is indeed rising. However, these childrens' utility as a source of productive labour to augment the family income (b) and their utility as a source of security to offset the income drop at the end of the parents' productive life (c) both decline. On the other hand, the direct cost of each child increases, since, he assumes, the effect of rising income is to promote a desire for what economists refer to as 'higher quality' children. 'The new occupational environment limits opportunities for child labour, requires more costly training for children, and necessitates smaller family obligations on the part of the parents so that they can take advantage of new and different economic opportunities'. Further, the indirect costs of children increase in the sense that there is a greater opportunity cost involved in looking after them (d).

Leibenstein makes two important qualifications of detail to this general model. First, he suggests that as infant mortality declines at the beginning of the transitional period, so the number of expected child-utility years increases, and with it the desired and so the actual number of children. Eventually, it will be realised that the costs of caring for this extra load outweigh the ultimate benefits, and the fertility rate will then decline. This temporary rise and fall he terms 'the infant mortality hump'. Second, he argues that the most important determinant of fertility in the last period of the transition will be the cyclical fluctuations of the mature, industrial economy, whether they are long (so-called 'Kuznets cycles') or short (more usually referred to as 'business cycles').

The first of these two qualifications, together with the general model, is supported by a recent calculation of Lorimer's (1967). Lorimer constructs models from six variables, the level and pattern of fertility, the level of mortality, consumption needs by sex and age, production potentials by sex and age, the relation of the nuclear family to other social structures, and productive resources, to simulate the following conditions: (i) traditional agriculture, high fertility, and high mortality; (ii) the same, except for moderate mortality; (iii) early industrialisation, high fertility, and moderate mortality; and (iv) the same, except for moderate fertility. His calculations therefore apply solely to the early period of transition. High fertility he takes to be 7·0, moderate 4·0; ages at marriage in the first three conditions are 18 for women and 21 for men, and are postponed five years for the fourth; it is assumed that children leave the parental family at marriage; and it is assumed that the first birth occurs after an interval of 1·0— 1·9 years, successive intervals being of 2, 3, 3, 3, 3, and 4 years. Female expectations of life at birth are taken to be thirty years (high mortality) or fifty years (moderate mortality). Lorimer further assumes, from some Indian and Filipino data, that if an adult male consumption unit is taken as 1·0, an adult female's will be 0·8 and that those of children of both sexes will be 0·3 under two years' old, rising by equal amounts to 0·4 at five and thereafter by larger amounts to the adult level at fifteen years. He remarks that this scale may be conservative. He takes the relative productivity values under traditional agriculture as 1·6 adult male consumption units (males) and 0·8 units (females), with children of both sexes only contributing 0·15 at eight years, rising to a mean of the adult level (1·2) at 15 years. Half the children reaching 18, that is, the males, remain at home for another 3 years. Under early industrialisation, male productivity rises to 1·8, female drops to 0·6 (giving the same couple=productivity as in agriculture). Children reach 0·12 at 12 years, rising to the mean level (1·2) at 15. He remarks again that this too may be conservative, in underestimating agriculture-industry differences.

From these assumptions, which rest on contemporary demographic observations and a few surveys, Lorimer calculates that under the first set of conditions, there is a net surplus of production-consumption units of 14·34. The period of deficit during the stage of family formation is for eleven years but only amounts to −2·16 units. Under the second set, the surplus drops to 12·52, and the deficit period, also eleven years, amounts to −4·79 units. It is under the third set of conditions that the greatest stress occurs. There, the overall surplus becomes an overall deficit, of −11·07 units, and the intermediate deficit period has extended to twenty-three years and −19·08 units. Finally, a net surplus re-emerges, albeit a small one (2·56 units), and the deficit period drops back to fifteen years and −10·59 units. In this last stage, the delayed age at marriage does not affect production-consumption relations 'but changes their location in the family cycle'.

These calculations are hypothetical, in that they do not relate to one observed population. Lorimer has assembled data of various kinds from various societies and analysed their interactions in one model. Nevertheless, there is already some evidence that for presently developing societies this model, and thus Leibenstein's too, does correspond to reality (Gupta and Malaker, 1963). Whether or not it also makes the historical transitions intelligible is less certain. These transitions differ among themselves, and economic historians and historical demographers cannot often agree on what exactly happened *within* one society (see Krause, 1967; Razzell, 1965; 1967; and Habbakuk, 1955 for Britain; Petersen, 1960 for the Netherlands; as well as other historical material referred to in earlier chapters and Wrigley, 1969).

There is, however, one crucial assumption behind Leibenstein's and Lorimer's work that cannot be evaded. This is that economic growth is, or was, largely independent of and prior to any demographic transition. Economists, economic historians and demographers still do not agree about this, although there is at present a conventional wisdom, well summarised by Ohlin (1967), which would justify the assumption. 'By and large', Ohlin decides, 'the growth of population in the past must to a large extent have been a response to economic advance in a broad sense. Instances of 'population pressure' undoubtedly occurred, but the broad sweep of growth is more easily interpreted as a consequence of the opening up of new territories and industries'.[2] On the other hand, the growth of population in modern under-developed and developing societies has occurred much more swiftly and at a different stage in the process of economic advance, and the Leibenstein-Lorimer approach can only be justified on the assumption that these societies, despite their chronic demographic difficulties, can nevertheless manage to achieve some economic growth *before* population growth begins to decelerate. Such an assumption, of course, begs one of the most crucial questions in the political economy of the presently developing nations. All one can say is that if economic growth does emerge, then these sorts of mechanisms will gradually come into play. All of which is not to deny the possibility of a reverse process, the possibility of couples deliberately limiting their families to a size below that necessary to maintain their standard of living and thus creating a surplus for investment of various kinds.

[2]For a fuller discussion of the issues and arguments, see, for example, the papers in United Nations (1967); Clark (1967); and Meade (1968), as well as Ohlin (1967).

Most economic historians are sceptical of this (see the excellent discussion in Wrigley, 1969), but whether or not family limitation was always practiced to balance resources or sometimes to increase them must remain a fundamental question for economic and demographic history.[3]

(b) Some Aggregative Studies

Some consequences of economic development for fertility are suggested, although by no means proved, by a series of aggregative statistical studies on various developing and developed societies. These have the advantage of referring to actual rather than hypothetical populations, but the considerable double disadvantage of only being carried out at one point in time and, because of their aggregative nature, of not demonstrating the nature of the mechanisms of family formation at the microscopic level. Three of them, Weintraub (1962), Adelman (1963) and Russett *et al.* (1964), found a positive relationship between per capita income (GNP divided by population size) and birth rates for a large sample of nations, results which conflict with the familiar long-term negative association between these two factors. A further study (Friedlander and Silver, 1967) found a positive relationship for developed countries only, but a negative one for those 'with no clear evidence of self-sustaining [economic] growth'. In another, Heer (1966) set out to test the hypothesis that the direct effect of a rise in the per capita income on fertility was positive, but that such a rise is but one aspect of development in general, other aspects of which serve to depress fertility and so counteract the income effect. His regressions are not inconsistent with this thesis, and those of the other workers can also be interpreted in this way (with the exception of Friedlander and Silver). Heer accounts for the small positive relationship between income and fertility (partial correlation coefficients of ·102 in an additive model and ·037 in a multiplicative one) in terms of the supposedly strong countereffect of high fertility on economic development, a causal process that is confounded with any in the reverse direction in a simple correlation coefficient. He would presumably explain Friedlander and Silver's negative relationship by

[3] I owe this crucial point, like many others in economic history, to Eric Jones.

saying that the reverse, adverse effect of fertility on GNP had happened to dominate in their sample of least developed nations. It is also perhaps no coincidence that the latest of such studies finds that the situation in developing societies has changed since the earlier ones were carried out. Friedlander and Silver's own explanation is that a standardisation for levels of economic development, a feature of their study, may reduce the variation in apparent income elasticities.

The two aspects of development that Heer considers to have the strongest counter-effect to rising fertility under conditions of rising income are public health measures to reduce infant mortality and the level of education. Again his, and the others', results bear him out. Friedlander and Silver, however, find a negative relationship between education and fertility only when that education has extended over a period of some years. They find no such association between mere literacy and fertility, literacy presumably being possible at an educational threshold well below that considered necessary, if not sufficient, to adopt the kind of rationality and orientation to the future that make for successful birth planning and control.

One other aggregative, statistical period study is of interest (Adelman and Morris, 1965–66). These two applied factor-analytic techniques to crude fertility rates and 'a large number of indices representing the social and political structure of 55 less-developed countries in the period 1957–62', on the grounds that the searching function of factor analysis would be valuable in a field of inquiry in which there were no well-developed theoretical models from which testable hypotheses might be generated. These grounds are somewhat naive for someone working in the 1960s, and it is not surprising that Adelman and Morris arrive at the point reached by more speculative workers a decade or so before, albeit by an apparently rigorous route and so are able to put precise weights to the associations that they discover. Their twenty-four socio-political indicators accounted, in their model, for 57 per cent of the inter-state fertility differences, and of this 57 per cent, half was accounted for by the factor that included the indicators of the size of the agricultural sector, the type of family structure, the literacy rate, the extent of mass communications, the degree of ethnic and cultural homogeneity, the significance of an indigenous middle class, the degree of modernisation of outlook of the states' leaders and the type of religion (according to the extent to which it emphasised the individual's control over his own fate).[4] The inclusion of GNP per capita explained no more variance, it being very highly correlated indeed with this first combined factor. Their conclusion is thus similar to Ryder's (see above; 1959): the more modern a nation, by the usual social and political indicators, the lower its crude fertility rate. But is is debatable as to what extent the apparent precision of their statistical measures of communality adds to this general conclusion. Adelman and Morris's paper, largely because it resorts to factor analysis to search for hypotheses, rather than to more conventional regression techniques to test ones generated elsewhere, is less successful than those by Weintraub, Russett, Heer, Freidlander and Silver and indeed than Adelman's own earlier one. All such studies can only be extremely crude pointers to the validity or otherwise of hypotheses which depend for more conclusive testing on quite different, and specifically more micro and less macro, data.

Leibenstein's second qualification, that in the last period of the demographic transition the main determinant of fertility and marriage rates will be cyclical fluctuations in the economy, was supported by one outstanding study when he wrote (Galbraith and Thomas, 1941), and has since been corroborated by others (Kirk and Nortman, 1958; Kirk, 1960; Silver, 1965; 1965–66). Two cross-sectional studies, however, have found no relation between recessions or booms and fertility (Westoff *et al.*, 1963; Freedman and Coombs, 1966b). Thomas pointed out that the persistence of correlations of between ·70 and ·90 between business cycles and marriage rates 'is perhaps, one of the most firmly based empirical findings in any of the social sciences' (comment to Kirk, 1960). Silver's recent work on the United States, the United Kingdom and Japan did not produce quite such startling associations (the coefficients of determination were of the order of ·50), but they are still good. The association with fertility is less strong, and its absence in the two cross-sectional studies suggests that business cycles may have their strongest effect on

[4]The exact indicators used for these general concepts can be found in appendices to the paper.

marriage rates and first-parity births. In short, they are perhaps determinants of the timing rather than of the quantity of vital events, although of course if a recession delays the reproductive behaviour of couples in which the wife is towards the higher end of the child-bearing period then there might well be an effect on total fertility. Work at present in progress in the United States suggests this (Campbell, 1967), and Ryder (1969) implies that this was the effect of the relative depression before the Second World War. Easterlin's empirical work, discussed above (1962; 1966), has been on the impact of longer Kuznets cycles, and in it he has made the necessary connections (still at present hypothetical) between the aggregate events and the micro-economics and micro-sociology of which those events are the intellectual construction. He sees economic conditions working in part *via* the income effect and in part *via* preferences by shaping primarily material aspirations during adolescence. This is slightly at variance with some earlier studies of the relationship between business cycles and fertility, in which it was assumed that the effect was achieved through the impact of fluctuations in the rate of unemployment. There is no direct evidence for this assumption and indeed the second of the two published Princeton reports (Westoff *et al.*, 1963) reveals that those couples most affected by a recession that happened to fall between the two surveys were more likely to be contraceptively effective anyway, thus nullifying, if not actually reversing, the expected relationship. More affected in the expected direction were those groups of higher status.

(c) *The Example of Income*

However, several sociologists have assumed that since there is no direct relationship between income and fertility in recent cross-sectional (as distinct from time series) studies, so that hypothesis too must be discarded (see especially Blake, 1967; 1968). A glance at the findings of both the Princeton and the Growth of American Families studies would seem to bear out this scepticism, and it is also corroborated by some census data from other societies (see, for instance, the data for West Germany reported by Clark, 1967). Blake's argument, for example, is simple. Once fertility control has become 'diffused' evenly through an industrial society, one would expect a positive relationship between income and ideal, desired, expected or actual fertility. She takes this point of departure from Becker (1960). However, she points out such a positive relationship does not exist. Indeed (and excepting for the moment Catholics, who constitute a comprehensible special case in this respect), there is virtually no relationship at all. The income-fertility hypothesis, she thus concludes, must be abandoned. She adduces additional circumstantial evidence to suggest that the crucial determinants are rather much more straightforwardly sociological, in that they have to do with non-economic norms.

This argument misunderstands the sophisticated economic thesis and the misunderstanding is revealed by some other evidence of the impact of income on fertility in both advanced and developing, or undeveloped, societies. It is brought out in Easterlin's own argument against Becker (see above; 1969). Easterlin insists that the effect of income must be seen as the effect also of tastes, preferences or norms for the disposal of that income. 'Per capita income growth', he suggests, 'operates through two channels. On the one hand, it has the effect usually emphasised of tending to increase fertility by giving the second generation more resources. On the other, it tends to lower fertility by increasing the relative desire for material goods. Since these two influences may be more or less offsetting, it no longer follows that per capita income growth tends to increase fertility secularly'. It does not, however, follow from this that one may ignore the income variable altogether. The nature and extent of the offsetting process is an empirical question to be determined afresh for each sample studied.

Evidence for Easterlin's argument is of two kinds. First is that bearing directly on tastes. Freedman and Coombs (1966b) found in a 1961 Detroit sample that there was an inverse relationship between fertility expectations and aspirations for children. They also found that when income expectations (a rough measure of potential or permanent income) were matched against fertility expectations, there was a positive relation. It follows from this, although it was not directly tested, that the highest fertility would be likely to accrue to those whose income rose over time but whose tastes did not, and that the lowest would accrue to those whose tastes did rise but whose income did not. Similar findings have emerged from an English pilot study (Hawthorn and Busfield, 1968). Secondly, there is indirect evidence which may be interpreted to measure the effect of tastes. Deborah Freedman (1963) found that an income above the mean for the husband's occupation, age and educational status was conducive to more children than was normal for the values on these latter three dimensions with the mean income, and that when the income fell below the mean, there were fewer children. 'Being in a higher absolute income class', she adds, 'means fewer children if the higher income is only what is usual for the husband's age and occupational status'. This interesting finding is corroborated from some old Swedish census data, in which income and occupation were cross-tabulated for fertility (Hyrenins 1946). Stys (1957–58), in his deservedly famous article on the effect of holding-size on the fertility of peasants in southern Poland (birth cohorts 1885–1929), noticed that the absolute values of the relative differences between the richer peasants, with higher fertility, and the poorer ones, with lower fertility, were lower in those villages near towns. This implies some impact of tasts spreading out from the urban zone to the rural settlements. The steady differential between the richer and the poorer peasants, steady in its direction if not its magnitude, would lead one on the present hypothesis to assume that tastes were more nearly constant across all peasant strata. The upturn in fertility among the land*less* peasants is explained by Stys as the effect of their guaranteed employment as labourers on large estates. Easterlin himself quotes work by Goldberg (1959; 1960) and Duncan (1965) to show that the more positive relation that emerges between income and fertility when farm background and education are controlled might indicate that once taste-forming factors have been eliminated, the relationship is as expected. Duncan's work on the Indianapolis data (1964) also supports this. [5] However,

---

[5]Goldberg's (1960) and Duncan's (1964) reinterpretations of the 1941 Indianapolis data (see Whelpton and Kiser (eds.), 1946, 1950, 1952, 1954, 1958) are open to the contamination of income classes in those data by differential, and associated, planning success. See Blake (1968).

the study of background variables assumed or known from other sociological and social-psychological studies to be determinants of attitudes, norms, tastes or whatever can only be a second-best alternative to the kind of inquiry conducted by Freedman and Coombs (1966b).

A further problem involved in examining the relationship between income and fertility, and which may at first sight seem merely technical, is that of measuring income. Quite apart from the distinction between income and wealth, and no study to my knowledge has yet looked thoroughly at *both* together, there is the question of current versus past and potential (or permanent) income. Freedman and Coombs (1966a; 1966b) and Deborah Freedman (1963) took this into account, but most of the commoner cross-sectional studies have taken a cross-sectional view of income. This is likely to be a particularly severe distortion for those couples, usually in middle and upper status-groups, whose income typically rises more or less steadily over time, especially when those couples are observed at the beginning of their married lives. Taking a simple view of the costs involved in bringing up children (see the discussion of Leibenstein, above), Mincer (1963) has attempted to examine the effect of *foregone* potential income on fertility. Making Becker's assumption that when contraceptive efficiency in a population is high, fertility will respond to income in the direct way that classical demand theory suggests (an assumption already criticised, but which does not vitiate the interest of the analysis), Mincer regresses husband's and wife's income onto fertility for a sample of 400 families from a 1950 survey of consumer expenditurees in which the wife was between 35 and 45. He finds a positive effect of husband's income outweighed by a negative effect of wife's income: the former is 0·10, the latter 0·19. His inference is that the wife's income represents the opportunity cost of children to her, a cost that outweighs the benefit of the income itself which, taken alone, might be expected to show the positive effect on fertility of the husband's income. These results can be further interpreted to contradict Mincer's original assumption from Becker (1960) that income and fertility are directly related, since it is likely that as the husband's income rises, so does that of the wife (given the high degree of assortative mating in all societies). Since the latter income measures the opportunity cost of children to the wife (if not to the couple), the upshot is likely to be the lack of a clear relation between income and fertility: just as we have found from other cross-sectional studies. Perhaps the conclusion to studies of the income effect must be that independent of changing tastes, income is directly related to fertility, but that tastes are rarely independent, and thus that the observed relationships are likely to vary within narrow limits around the measure of no association. Perhaps one can conclude by suggesting that the positive effect of income over time will be marked but temporary as tastes, which characteristically lag behind, catch up.

Five points may be made about this work on the association between income and fertility. First, income is the factor most obviously related to economic development, and thus to the main theses about the causes of the various demographic transitions in various societies. Secondly, however, it has been relatively neglected by students of fertility. This can only partly be explained by the very considerable practical difficulties involved in obtaining information about it. Thirdly, and also related to the relative paucity of relevant information, is the fact that it is deceptively difficult to measure. This does not apply, of course, to the more usual notion of current income, but to the more meaningful one of permanent or potential income. Fourthly, and more important, income has frequently been adduced without sufficient attention to the way in which it might affect behaviour generally and fertility in particular. The same might be said of the complementary concept of norms (see, for instance, the otherwise useful review by Ronald Freedman, 1963). These are special cases of my argument in Chapters IV and VI. Fifthly, lastly, and for sociologists most importantly, the complexity of the demonstrated income effects on fertility is a powerful argument in itself against the more embracing measures of social position that sociologists commonly use. A simple association between, say, something called 'socio-economic status' and fertility can be interpreted in a variety of ways. At its simplest, it could be measuring the effects of class rather than status (in the Weberian senses of those terms). At its most complex, it could be measuring the effects, some of them contradictory, of a host of factors: absolute and relative income and wealth, occupational security, occupational and community prestige or status, educational experience, consumption patterns and so forth. The offsetting effects of income and tastes for material and social advancement which the literature I have just discussed appears to reveal would be quite lost within the great majority of standard social class or socio-economic status measures. Occasionally, as for example in Rainwater's study, one can gather information on one of the class dimensions, but such accidents depend upon the extensive reporting of qualitative interviews and usually do not appear in tabulations. It is inadequate to have to hope for, rather than expect, such precision.

3 INDEPENDENT VARIABLES IN GENERAL

(a) *Their Conceptualisation*

To the argument (in Chapters II—IV) that 'fertility' is the function of the interaction between the three components of fecundity, intervening demographic factors and fertility intentions, is thus now addded the parallel one that there can be no simple-minded conceptualisation of the independent variables. I have argued this by example, using the concept of income as one dimension of social class or socio-economic status. The point may be made another way, using Stinchcombe's (1968) illuminating analogy with type-concepts in other sciences. If a type-concept is defined as a concept which is constructed from a combination of the values of several variables, it is clear that, for example, the chemical elements are satisfactory type-concepts, and that social classes are not. A chemical element typically displays a consistent profile of values across the variables of valence, atomic weight, boiling and freezing points, specific gravity at a given temperature, number of atoms in a molecule, and the strength of the bond it forms in compounds. It is therefore possible to talk of something called 'hydrogen' and know that it will always display the same set of values across all variable dimensions. Such is not the case with social class. In one situation, there will be one profile, in another a different one. Were this not so, the sociological attention long given to multi-dimensional rank measures as an empirical problem would have been unnecessary.

(b) The Example of Social Class

It follows from this fairly obvious point that simple associations between, say, socio-economic status and fertility are going to be far too crude for causal analysis. Each of the two concepts has to be broken down into its variable components, and the relationship between the value of any one variable and any other be made a matter for empirical investigation. Thus, the relatively plentiful data on differential fertility by social class or socio-economic status can at best *specify* the questions that we need to ask; they can never *answer* explanatory questions. Summaries of such data appear in Wrong (1958b; 1960), Johnson (1960), Kiser (1960) and Glass (1968), as well as in a multitude of smaller studies listed in the bibliography, and in national censuses. They show that the historical decline in the birth rate was characterised by a gradual development of an inverse relationship between fertility and socio-economic status and by a broadening of differentials. Progress towards lower fertility was more rapid in urban than rural areas. The differentials were largely the result of differences in the rate of decline. It was expected that as the initial decline spread to all statuses and all areas, there would be a convergence of differentials. This has, to some extent, occurred. The fertility of the lowest socio-economic groups is now considerably lower than it was in the earlier stages of industrialisation. But the fertility of the higher groups has increased since the Second World War in industrial societies, with the result that the prospective convergence has been stopped, or at least delayed. Instead, there is now something of a reverse 'J' or 'U' curve, with the lowest fertility among those of intermediate status and education. This is well illustrated by the latest differential fertility figures for England and Wales (General Register Office, 1966).

For marriages of 10 to 14 years' duration in 1961, marriages in which fertility is nearly complete, given what we know about present patterns of the timing of family formation in advanced societies, and excluding members of the armed forces and 'others', the highest mean family size is 2.30

(unskilled manual workers), the next highest 2·17 (self-employed professionals), and the lowest 1·68 (junior non-manual workers). The second of these three figures is something of a novelty, it not being apparent in 1951 (as is evident from the means for marriages of longer duration in 1961). No other non-manual mean reaches 2·00.

The recent rise in the completed family size, or, more precisely, *projected* completed family size, of self-employed professionals in England and Wales serves as a good example of the way in which such simple associations can only specify questions and not answers. The parallel mean for professional employees is only 1·86, and the new divergence prompts one to look for differences between these superficially similar occupational groups which might explain the differential fertility. So far, no one has done any systematic work on this particular problem (although the Institute of Community Studies in London have recently looked at a small sample of architects, but taking no control from professional employees), and the field for hypotheses is an open one. One suggestion is that the (presumably) highly-educated wives of the self-employed professional husbands suffer high opportunity costs in not working, and offset this loss with a deliberately high family. Another is that the relative income of this group is now considerably higher, and that they can therefore afford to have more children than others in their age, education and mobility classes. A third might be that the personal security afforded by the higher relative income, or by a higher status on other dimensions, induces relatively inefficient contraceptive practice. Or it may be that self-employed professional people have greater opportunities than their employed professional peers for a more rapid income-rise when young, and so get married earlier, thus exposing themselves to risk in a more fecund period (provided that the age at marriage does not drop to a very low level, under 19). One or more of these hypotheses could account for the observed differential, and they do not by any means exhaust the possible explanations. The opportunity for sociological imagination is large. But I have said enough to illustrate the point that simple socio-economic status/fertility associations can only specify questions and not provide answers.

Having stressed the importance of finer than usual distinctions among the conventional independent sociological variables,[6] illustrated this with a comparison between the concepts of income and socio-economic status, and restated the conditions for a satisfactory explanation of fertility differentials, I now wish to turn back to the components of the dependent variable and review the social determinants that have been suggested or demonstrated for each of them.

4 FECUNDITY

I know of no comprehensive work on the social determinants of fecundability (but see James, 1969). Understandably most attention has so far been devoted to measuring fecundability itself. In so far as fecundity is socially determined, it is affected through one or more of the intervening variables classified through one or more of the intervening variables classified by Davis and Blake (1956), and described in Chapter III. Leaving aside coital frequency, about which little is known, and involuntary fecundity factors and foetal mortality, there are nine relevant intervening variables: the age of entry into sexual unions, the proportion of women never entering sexual unions, the amount of the reproductive period spent after or between unions, voluntary abstinence from sexual intercourse, the use (or not) of contraception, the resort to sterilisation, subincision, etc., and voluntary foetal mortality. In addition to this set (see Davis and Blake, 1956) is voluntary infanticide, which affects ultimate family size if not fertility (a somewhat academic point in view of the fact that those societies in which infanticide still occurs are also those in which registration is poor, so that fertility has to be measured by the child-woman ratio or some other equally crude index).

5 MARRIAGE
(a) *Age at Marriage*
Less is probably known about the social determinants of the age at marriage and the proportions marrying than about the determinants of any other important demographic variable. Information is most glaringly absent for primitive societies. Conventional anthropological work on kinship and marriage does not seem much concerned with the age at marriage, nor

[6]'Than usual', that is, in other sociological research.

with the proportions marrying (see, for example, Coale, *et al.*, 1965; Fox, 1967), and thus gives few leads to their corre-lates. Nevertheless, it is not a subject about which it is difficult to speculate. In a kinship system of extended families, mar-riage does not necessarily imply the formation of a separate household (see the theoretical discussion by Coale in Coale, *et al.*, 1965; and Indian work by Driver, 1963; Mayer, 1960; Nag, 1967; Pakrasi and Malaker, 1967); in nuclear systems, on the other hand, it does. It follows that resource constraints on marriage are likely to be more severe in the latter system, and thus that the age at marriage, and even possibly the pro-portions ultimately marrying, will tend on average to be later in these systems. If this is so, one would expect this to have an adverse effect on fertility, as well as a positive effect on the accumulation of resources (or the ratio of productive resources to consumption), and thus on economic develop-ment, itself negatively related to fertility after the 'infant mortality hump' is passed.

The credibility of this reasoning is supported by the evi-dence for pre-industrial and industrial Europe on the one hand, and societies such as India on the other (see Chapter III). However, as Driver, Nag, Pakrasi and Malaker point out (and see also Blake, 1967b), under adverse conditions the early marriage in joint families in India and China is more *de jure* than *de facto*. Young couples are frequently separated in the joint household, so that coital frequencies are lower and the probability of conception correspondingly reduced. Such a mechanism may well account for the low coital fre-quencies that, for instance, Bourgeois–Pichat (1965a) assumes for this kind of society. Both Nag and Pakrasi and Malaker find that the fertility of couples living in joint households is lower than that of those in their own nuclear households. This contradicts the suggestions of earlier workers (Davis, 1955; Lorimer, 1954).

Blake (1967b) has attacked the problematic relationship between kinship systems and the age at marriage from a rather different point of view. Rather than classifying societies by the degree of nuclearity of their family structures, she distinguishes between those structures within which marriages are arranged and those within which there is a relatively free choice of marital partner. She hypothesised that the age at marriage in the former would be significantly lower than that in the latter. The hypothesis is only partially confirmed, since, from the admittedly scanty evidence that she is able to adduce, it appears that arranged marriages can either be very early or very late. It is more likely that free marriages will take place between these extremes. The dichotomy is thus not a good one for distinguishing between kinship factors in the determination of the age at marriage.

Much more fruitful are hypotheses relating resources to the age at marriage. Indeed, it is not unlikely, if the sort of reasoning that I have suggested above applies, that the kin systems themselves are dependent on the supply of resources. The work on the relationship between economic cycles and reproductive factors that I discussed earlier in this chapter shows indisputably that marriage rates, and thus the age at marriage, are strongly affected by economic fluctuations; moreover, this appears to be true for several otherwise different cultures (Silver, 1965–66). Other evidence, such as Wrigley's on the Devon village of Colyton in the seventeenth century, that on Ireland, and Banks' work on the Victorian middle classes in England, supports this, and it may indeed be true, as Coale (1967) suggests, that nuptiality control was the clearest response to changing economic conditions before and during the early stages of the demographic transition. Later, as methods of birth control became more familiar and effective, the restraint on marriage was relaxed in favour of intramarital contraception. Ryder (1969) and others have plausibly hypothesised that the recent decline in the age at marriage is less something new than a swing back to the trend observable up to the 1920s, and interrupted by the relatively severe economic situation in the West up to the late 1930s. He adds that, given a higher proportion of young people staying on longer in full-time education in these societies, it is likely that the age at marriage will not irreversibly drop any lower, but rather than the future will see fluctuations around a level trend dependent upon temporary economic recessions and booms. In short, marriage is extremely sensitive to economic conditions, but this sensitivity declines as the availability and efficiency of methods of birth control increase.

One simple inference, however, from this observation does not seem to be borne out by the evidence. This is that, given that the availability and efficiency of contraception is lower in lower classes (see below), and given that these classes are economically less advantaged (by definition) than those above them, it should follow that they have a higher age at marriage. But the reverse seems to be true. One explanation for this might be that the desire to maintain their relatively higher allocation of scarce and desirable resources prompts the middle class to take similar delaying action in conditions of economic difficulty. And it does appear from American and British work (Rele, 1965; Grebenik and Rowntree, 1963) that this is the case. The decline in the age at marriage in Britain, for example, since 1945 has apparently taken place in all social classes, although it is still true that it is slightly later in the middle class than in the working class.

The two recent American surveys have differed in their findings of the correlates of the age at marriage. The Princeton study found no significant differentials by socio-economic status or religion; the G.A.F. study, on the other hand, found that the middle class and Catholics tended to marry later, although the differences were not very large. All groups, as Rele has shown, took part in the decline in the age of marriage in the late 1940s and 1950s. The impact of the religious differential on births is not, however, proportional to the difference in the age at marriage betwen them. This is because Catholics tend to have their children at shorter intervals, so offsetting the demographic effect normally expected from a later age at marriage. Both studies, however, point up the status of the age at marriage as a truly intervening variable between social factors and fertility; both show a strong association between an early age at marriage, shorter birth intervals, a larger desired family size, and higher ultimate fertility, and this bundle tends to be associated more with the lower socio-economic groups. The reasons for this are discussed below, in considering the determinants of contraceptive practice and fertility intentions.

(b) Interruption and Dissolution
It was long suggested that the prohibition on widow-re-

marriage in certain societies, and particularly India, had a dampening effect on fertility. The demographic evidence (Chapter III above) does not support this, it being apparently more common for a woman to re-marry unless she is at the end of her fecund period (and thus old), in which case the death of the husband will not have affected fertility anyway. The Caribbean situation of consensual unions, a matrilocal social organisation in which genitors come and go at fairly frequent but irregular intervals, does, however, seem to depress fertility, and the reasons are obvious: such an interrupted exposure to the risk of conception occurs during the most fecund period. I know of no evidence, however, to suggest that either prohibitions on remarriage or the prevalence of consensual unions have been invoked or encouraged deliberately to control fertility. One might nevertheless wish to invoke an argument to the effect that both institutions *have the function of* depressing fertility, and further that they must both therefore meet some need in the societies in which they occur. I personally am sceptical of such arguments, unless it can be shown that did such institutions not exist, the society would suffer serious dysfunctions. I do not think that this could be argued in these cases.

6   BIRTH CONTROL

(a) *Abstinence*

For the same reasons that little can be usefully said about the incidence and effect of coital frequencies on fertility, so there is little to say about voluntary abstinence. It is fairly clear that certain cultures, such as Islam, place a higher value on sexual relationships within marriage than do others, such as Christianity; and it may well be that such differences are later expressions of different ecological exigencies in the history of the relevant societies, and that they have their origins in historical attempts to control or stimulate population growth. But I know of no evidence to settle such questions. It is, in fact, perhaps not too evasive to say that relatively little sociological attention needs to be paid to the factor of voluntary abstinence, since its demographic effects are probably small compared with those of other intervening variables.

(*b*) *Contraception*
Such, of course, is not the case with contraception. Together
with the age at marriage and the proportions marrying, which
determine the number of woman-years at risk in a population, birth control and related practices probably account
for the larger part of the variance in family size in all societies. I say the 'larger part' and not 'most' advisedly: it may
well be, as Westoff *et al.* (1961) and Bodmer and Jacquard
(1968) have suggested, that nearly half of the variance of
achieved family size among married couples may be accounted
for by non-motivational factors. This observation re-affirms
the crucial importance of discussions of natural fertility in
understanding that amount of fertility that is amenable to
non-biological explanations.

The single most important finding of the determinants of
contraceptive use and effectiveness is that both increase as the
desired family size is reached (Westoff *et al.*, 1963). In other
words, extent of use and effectiveness is a function of the
motivation to stop at a particular parity. As the authors of
The Third Child point out, quoting a remark of Freedman's,
this reconciles the findings of high failure rates with, for example, the successful limitation of families during periods of
economic recession without having to invoke extraordinary
abortion or sterilisation rates. It also serves as a warning to
those who may observe low use and high failure in a sample
of women who have not yet reached their desired family sizes.
The extent to which this generalisation applies across cultures
is, however, unclear. Hill, Stycos and Back (1959) report that
many of their lower-class sample did not resort to freely
available sterilisation even when they had passed their expressed desired family size. Two interpretations of this are
possible: either that the Princeton generalisation does not
hold, or the expressed desires were not held with any conviction. Given the extent of fatalism in such populations, the
second seems more probable. Contrary evidence is available
from, for example, some other Latin American studies, where
the resort to abortion increases dramatically as the desired
family size is reached, regardless of the religious affiliation
and devotion of the mothers (Miro, 1966). Davis (1967),
among others, has commented on the implications of this

7

finding. Providing, he argues, that the motivations to achieve and not exceed the average desired family size of four children in developing societies is strong enough, there will be little problem in encouraging the prospective parents to adopt effective contraceptives. The real problem lies in lowering the desires themselves. Whether this can be done until the kinds of constraints that Leibenstein and Lorimer describe begin to operate, constraints commonly felt to be consequent upon rather than prior to fertility decline, is another—as yet undecided—question.

Moreover, Davis' assumption that, providing the motivations are strong enough, there will be little problem in persuading prospective parents to adopt effective contraception is rather too optimistic. This is because although a strong motivation to achieve a particular family size is a necessary condition of contraceptive effectiveness, it is not sufficient. To understand this it is necessary to make more explicit a remark I made in Chapter IV, when discussing Rainwater's work: namely, that a satisfactory explanation of fertility intentions will have to be accompanied by an account of those factors that prevent such conscious desires from being reached. The point becomes clearer if a four-fold typology is suggested. On one axis is the distinction between strong and weak or negligible intentions; on the other the distinction between those couples who have the resources to effectively realise those intentions, and those who do not.

The factors other than income that affect intentions are discussed below; here I wish to examine those affecting actual contraceptive use and effectiveness. To begin with, and as one would expect, the basic resource of knowledge of contraceptive methods varies enormously across and within societies. Such knowledge is also changing rapidly, and it is thus pointless for me to summarise any reported figures here. However, it is true of all societies that awareness of methods of birth control varies directly with urban background or residence, a higher than average education, and a higher than average income (see the American and British studies discussed in III, above; also Caldwell, 1966; Hawley and Prachuabmoh, 1966; Kirk, 1967; Morsa, 1966; for information on Egypt, Ghana, Lebanon, Thailand, Turkey and Tunisia). And nearly always, it is those parents aged between 25 and 39 who are more aware than younger and especially older ones. Empirically, of course, it is difficult to separate the resource of knowledge from the strength of the motivation to control fertility: the latter is clearly a cause of acquiring the former. Nevertheless, the fact remains that couples may not be able to make use of such knowledge below a particular threshold of education.

Knowledge alone, however, even assuming it to be directly associated with motivation, is not sufficient for contraceptive success. Studies in urban America (Rainwater, 1960; 1965), England (Hawthorn and Busfield, 1968), France (Michel, 1967), Ghana (Caldwell, 1966), Israel (Matras and Auerbach, 1962) and Puerto Rico (Hill, Stycos and Back, 1959) have all found a comparatively strong connection between aspects of marital interaction and effectiveness. Hill, Stycos and Back, in their intensive study of the Puerto Rican lower class, were the first to successfully explore the area (the older Indianapolis Study had not found any strong associations), and concluded that 'communication (between parents) and time of perception of problems of family size[7] are by far the most important factors predicting competence and success in fertility control'. This is strikingly corroborated by Michel's French research:

TABLE XI

		Eradication of excess fertility	
		Puerto Rico	France
Couple agreement ..	..	·10	·53
Couple communication	..	·87	·52
Freedom (Puerto Rico)	..	·25	—
Dominance (France)	..	—	·36

Source: Michel (1967).

[7]See the discussion of the motivation-effectiveness function, above.

Rainwater's remarkable American work on the nature and effects of marital interaction (1960) also supports this, and goes more deeply into the kind of communication that is necessary. He distinguishes between relationships of 'mutuality' and 'rejection', terms which refer to the nature of the sexual relationship between men and women. The former are characterised by mutual genital interest, co-operation and discussion; it is more likely that female appliances will be used by these couples, and used more consistently and rationally. The latter relationships are characterised by the wife's distaste for the sexual interest her man has in her, lack of co-operation and emotional distance; in these couples, it is more likely that there will be a sporadic use of male appliances, with little effectiveness. Given the apparent similarity between the Puerto Rican findings and Rainwater's, it is tempting to conclude that the Latin American notion of *machismo*[8] enters into the contraceptively relevant marital interactions in the former society. Hill and his co-workers considered and rejected this at first sight attractive and plausible hypothesis. Together with the variable of Catholicity, it turns out to have been one of the myths of the determination of human fertility in Latin America. This important refutation strengthens one's conviction that the inverse association between the segregation of marital roles and contraceptive effectiveness is a truly cross-cultural one, and given the amount of variance that several workers have found it to account for, an important one.[9]

Earlier, I suggested a fourfold typology of couples by intention and family planning success: strong intentions—adequate resources for control; strong intentions—inadequate resources; weak or negligible intentions—adequate resources; and weak or negligible intentions—inadequate resources. Even before

[8]Discussed in Hill, Stycos, Back (1959); Stycos (1968), *passim*.

[9]The important exception to this is the Princeton finding (Westoff *et al.*, 1961; 1963). Tables 100 and 101 in the second report illustrate the very weak associations discovered between marital adjustment factors and family planning success. However, the questions from which the adjustment index was constructed (see the first report, pp. 403–04) seem rather anodyne and unimaginative. Although disconfirming instances must not be treated lightly, I can think of no feature of the Princeton sample that might explain this anomaly, and am inclined to think that the adjustment index is not discriminating enough. The authors themselves agree that the measures may be inadequate.

considering the remainder of the evidence on the correlates of firm intentions, it is clear from what I have said about income that the first of these four is both understandable and to be expected. The empirical location of the remaining three must wait until an examination of the distribution of the intensity with which intentions are held. The social distribution of the resources available for family planning, on the other hand, becomes immediately apparent from this remarkably good association in Rainwater's sample, an association so good that even the small number of cases gives no serious cause for doubt:

TABLE XII

	Role relationships		
	Joint	*Intermediate*	*Segregated*
Upper middle class* (32)	88%	12%	—
Lower middle class (31)	42	58	—
*Upper lower class** *			
Whites (26)	19	58	23
Negroes (25)	12	52	36
*Lower lower class** *			
Whites (25)	4	24	72
Negroes (29)	—	28	72

Source: Rainwater, (1965).

*The social classes are defined primarily by the occupational class of the husband: professional or business; white collar; skilled and semi-skilled manual; and unskilled manual. **Whites and Negroes at each class level combined for test. $\chi^2 = 100\cdot34$ df$=6$ P$<\cdot0005$ T$=\cdot50$.

Now, given also the fact that 'the greatest differences between socio-economic groups in the use of contraception are found when couples are classified by the wife's education' (Whelpton, Campbell and Patterson, 1966), a finding corroborated in several other studies (for example, Lewis–Faning, 1949), and that there is a close association between educational and occupational levels in American society (Blau and Duncan, 1967), it is clear that the distributions of the two main resources necessary for adequate family planning are largely co-terminous. The poorly educated are more likely to be in the lower classes, and more likely, therefore, to suffer more segrated marital role relationships. However, it would still be dangerous to make excessive simplifications about a lower-class syndrome, to assume that class is after all a type-concept in Stinchcombe's sense, for such an assumption may well founder in the face of anomalous findings like that in the 1961 fertility tables for England and Wales (General Register Office, 1966), where the highest fertility by terminal education age of the parents occurs to those couples in which the husband left school by 15 but in which the wife continued to beyond 20. There is also the exception of Catholics, where the fit between desired and achieved family sizes is *least* in those families where the wife is highly educated (see, for example, Westoff *et al.*, 1963).

(c) Abortion

Information on, let alone an understanding of, the social and sociopsychological correlates of other methods of control, such as subincision, sterilisation, and induced foetal mortality (or abortion) is less good. However, from the descriptions of their incidence that I summarised in Chapter III, it is not difficult to infer them from what we know of the correlates of contraception. As with the latter, the resort to the more drastic methods increases with parity, and is disproportionately located either in populations where ordinary contraceptives are unavailable or poor, or in those parts of populations characterised by poverty and low education. The Eastern European countries, including Greece but excluding Albania, are instances of the former class; the poverty-stricken parts of Latin America of the latter. The incidence of abortion is a striking affirmation of the generalisation that in Catholic cultures (strictly distinct from *sub*-cultures: see Day, 1968), whether Chilean or Yugoslavian, Latin American or European, the Catholic value-system is subordinate to economic constraints in the determination of family limitation.

Such is the present state of knowledge of the social determinants of the intervening variables. We know most about the determinants of contraceptive usage and effectiveness which are, after all, increasingly the most important of such variables, and perhaps least about the determinants of the age at marriage and the proportions married, almost certainly the next most important. Many sociologists, working in many different fields, have lamented the poverty of information about marriage and the family. Students of fertility have more cause than most for such lament. When data is available, it tends to concentrate upon the social organisation of the already-married, and to neglect the crucial questions of who gets married and when.

7 DETERMINANTS OF TASTES AND INTENTIONS

In conclusion, I now turn to those social factors other than the supply of resources (income) which appear to have some effect on fertility intentions. In the context of the model that I proposed in Chapter IV, these factors, which include the level of education, religious belief and so forth, can be seen as determining tastes, or preferences, and thus as complementary to the supply of resources to indulge those tastes. There is, however, an alternative way of looking at the effect of several of these non-income variables. Consider, as an example, the question of the couple's involvement with an extended kin network. Such a network might be seen as claiming a resource apart from income which is positively related to the desired number of children: namely, time. As far as I know, time as a resource has not been investigated from the point of view of a determinant of fertility, and I can thus only raise its possible relevance immediately to discard it, adding that the interaction between the income constraint, the time constraint and tastes would be a fruitful topic for analysis.

(a) Religion

The difficulty with many of the socio-economic, social and

socio-psychological factors that can be seen as affecting tastes is that they are also strongly related to the supply of income. A well-educated couple is also likely to be a prosperous one. Several surveyors have not held income constant when tabulating fertility by education, and this practice makes for uncertain interpretations (see, for example, Whelpton, Campbell and Patterson, 1966). But perhaps the factor least dependent upon socio-economic status and yet strongly related to tastes for children is that of religious affiliation. Studies of fertility in both developing and developed societies and regions have found it to be well-related. The greatest differences appear between Muslims and others in the Middle East, Central Asia and the Indian sub-continent (Driver, 1963; Kirk, 1967; Mazur, 1967; Rizk, 1963; Yaukey, 1961). Indian studies have also pointed to the relatively high Hindu fertility (exceeded only by that of Moslem groups). In his excellent review of the social correlates of fertility among 36 ethnic groups in the U.S.S.R., Mazur (1967) also points to the high fertility of Buddhists. The exact interpretation of the meaning of these religious differentials is not easy. Given the fact that Moslem, Hindu and—to a lesser extent—Buddhist practises predominate in societies in which, for the reasons that I have already discussed in examining Leibenstein's thesis, there is a strong need for son survival under conditions of labour-intensive agriculture, it is dangerous to assume that religious affiliation has a truly *independent* effect on fertility. It may so happen that the religious prescriptions coincide with economic necessity, and that it is therefore possible to see both fertility and religion as dependent upon economic considerations. The causal problem is analogous to that presented by the famous Protestant Ethic thesis, and perhaps better left to sociologists more expert in the analysis of religious belief and behaviour than I am. However, it should in principle be possible to test the independence of religious affiliation by assembling cross-tabulations of fertility by both religion and economic resources (or some proxy variable). The hypothesis would predict that religious fertility differentials would decline in the same proportion in a transition from one economic base to another. Potentially useful data is provided by Yaukey in his study of Christians and Muslims in rural and urban Lebanon (1961):

TABLE XIII

			Total Fertility Rates*	
			Christian	*Muslim*
Rural uneducated	..	..	6·81	5·94
Urban uneducated	..	..	4·14	5·84
Urban educated	..	..	3·41	4·68

Source: Yaukey (1961).

*holding age at marriage constant.

Assuming that the economic base in the villages differed from that in the towns (Yaukey provides no detailed information about this), the hypothesis is not borne out. The decline from country to town is greater among Christians than among Moslems, and even after a period of education the Muslim resistance to lower fertility is strong. And by no means all of the differences can be attributed to the differential availability of birth control (differential *use* being a measure of motivation and thus irrelevant as a confounding factor in this argument). At first sight, evidence such as that provided by Mazur (1967) on the fertility differences among Eastern Orthodox groups would appear to be more favourable for the hypothesis. Eastern Orthodox fertility is generally below the median level of that in the U.S.S.R. as a whole, but there is one sub-group—the Eastern Orthodox Yakuts—in which it is startlingly high. As many as twenty children appear in Yakut families, and children are regularly purchased. The economic system is one of extremely labour-intensive agriculture. It is thus possible that the power of religious affiliation to act independently of economic circumstances is very limited. However, the Eastern Orthodox faith, like Protestantism in all but its extreme anabaptist forms, makes no strong prescriptions either way about fertility, and allows its ppractitioners to regulate their fertility according to other criteria. The conclusion can only be that until more is known about the inter-relations between religious belief and economic behaviour it is best to treat as independent of each other and thus to be surprised at interdependence, rather than by its absence.

For one developing area, Latin America, and leaving aside the statistically unimportant sects, the nature of the religious effect is similar to that in all advanced societies except Japan and the Soviet Union: it is that Roman Catholics have a generally higher fertility than other Christians or those with no expressed religious affiliation. Bearing in mind the Church's attitude towards forms of birth and population control apart from the so-called 'rhythm method', this might be thought to be explicable in terms of the differential use of contraception and abortion. Two observations give the lie to this simple expectation: the lack of difference in the incidence of abortion between Catholic and non-Catholic groups (see Chapter III and above), and the fact that in Rio de Janeiro and San José at least, Catholic fertility in those groups with five years or more of university education is *higher* than that of those groups who have experienced secondary education only (and in Rio, higher than those who have experienced only primary schooling), (Miro and Rath, 1965; Stycos, 1968). But, when Catholic doctrine is inspected more closely, these apparent anomalies are not anomalous at all. Not only does the Church proscribe birth control, but it actively prescribes large families. It would thus follow that those who have been exposed more to Roman Catholic doctrine are those likely to take its prescriptions more seriously. These are likely to be the more highly educated groups.

This reasoning is borne out directly in American findings. Judith Blake (1966; 1966–67) has documented the comparative ideal family sizes of Catholics and non-Catholics in the United States, and both the Princeton and Growth of American Families studies found a direct relationship between Catholic education and ideal, desired, expected and achieved family size. Catholic education below the high school level did not seem to have much effect, and the greatest impact was visible in those with a college education. These findings are corroborated in the more particular study by Westoff and Potvin (1966). Blake's ideal family size studies show in some cases a U-shaped relation, rather than a direct one. These Protestant-Catholic differentials do not, contrary to what several observers had predicted, seem to be lessening as Catholics become more similar in other respects to Protestants. The difference cannot be explained in terms of underlying socio-economic attributes.

Pursuing van Heek's (1956) hypothesis that Catholic fertility will be higher among those Catholics who are in a minority, Day (1968) considers the available information to show the natality of Catholic minorities in Australia, New Zealand, the United States, Canada, the United Kingdom, the Netherlands and Switzerland to be higher than that of the Catholic majorities in Argentina, France, Belgium, Luxembourg, Italy, Austria, Czechoslovakia and Hungary. The argument is that high Catholic fertility is partly a function of the letter of Catholic prescription, but also partly a function of the extent to which one feels it necessary to emphasise one's faith in a spiritually hostile culture. He presents no survey evidence to corroborate this, and it is apparent that some of his Catholic majorities, such as Czechoslovakia and Hungary, have a low fertility level more easily explicable in other ways. It may also be that Day is reporting the effects of higher Catholic educational levels in the first of the two groups. The hypothesis from van Heek remains an interesting one, but its relative implausibility needs to be countered by less indirect evidence.

There is no evidence in the literature that I know of which suggests that the higher fertility of highly-educated Catholics in industrial societies and the cities of Latin America is due not only to their greater awareness of and adherence to Roman doctrine but also to the fact that these couples are relatively prosperous and may be releasing marginal resources towards children rather than other expenditure. The thesis would be that intermediate Catholics, like all intermediate groups, are disproportionately constrained, or *feel* disproportionately constrained, by economic circumstances, and that it is only those at either end of the scale who are free from such perceived constraints. At either end of the stratification system, Catholics are more able to indulge their tastes than in the middle. But, whatever the exact explanation, the fact remains that to some extent religious affiliation is a 'taste' factor not contaminated seriously by resource variables.

(b) Education

This is less certain for educational level. I have already mentioned the well-known direct relationship between educational level and contraceptive usage and effectiveness, and without sophisticated cross-tabulations it would be difficult to ascertain the impact of education on fertility intentions were the relationship between fertility and education an inverse one. Unfortunately, it is, or nearly always so. Both the Princeton and Growth of American Families studies found a direct, although somewhat weak, relationship between fertility and education. The stronger positive relationship between education and contraceptive effectiveness suggests that the total, and inverse, correlation may mask a small positive relationship between education and fertility intentions (see Blake, 1967 c). Recent British evidence supports this. The new differential between self-employed professionals and professional employees, which appeared in 1961 (see above; and General Register Office, 1966), cannot reasonably be attributed to differences in contraceptive effectiveness, and a glance at the tables of fertility by the terminal education age of the parents shows that, with the exception of those few couples in which the husband's education stopped at seventeen or below and the wife's continued until after twenty, the highest fertility fell to those couples in which *both* partners had been in full-time education up to and beyond the age of twenty. The suggestion is that a change in tastes is occurring at this level, and it may well be that the very slight upturn with education noticed in the second Growth of American Families study (Whelpton, Campbell and Patterson, 1966) will become more prominent in American data in the future. Quite how one explains this new pattern is unclear. Unfortunately, there are no cross-tabulations for England and Wales to assess the extent to which income differences may account for the educational difference. Until such tabulations are provided, it would be gratuitous to explain the new tastes until such time as one is certain that they are in fact new tastes, and not relatively greater resources flowing into couples with the same tastes (see the discussion of Easterlin's work, above, for similar arguments).

In view of the fact that American thinking in particular has tended to emphasise the probable effect of education on social aspirations, arguing that it raises the demand for goods and indeed introduces a demand for hitherto undesired ones, thus putting new pressures on income (itself, of course, also increasing with educational level), it is a pity that no fertility study has so far attempted to measure the effect of education on fertility *through tastes*. Despite the great detail provided in the most comprehensive studies, the fact remains that the correlations between education and fertility variables still leave the exact causal mechanisms somewhat obscure.

(c) Female Employment

Judith Blake (1965) and Davis (1967) have together argued that if fertility reduction is to be the goal of population policy, especially in developing countries, then encouraging couples to limit their fertility to their expressed desires will not be enough. The desires themselves have to be lowered. One way of doing this, Blake maintains, would be to demonstrate the advantages of gainful employment to the mothers. Qualifying her confidence by admitting that the direction of the causal relationship is not always clear, she nevertheless asserts that the 'association between married women working and family size is generally acknowledged to be one of the strongest, most persistent over time and space, and most theoretically reasonable' in the field of the social determinants of fertility. A close inspection of the literature, much of it published since she wrote this, leads to greater caution: all that can safely be said is that there does not seem to be a recorded instance in which there is a positive relationship between working women and fertility. But it is by no means always negative.

To begin with, and as she admits, there is a considerable proportion of working women who seek employment as a result of subfecundity. The second Growth of American Families study (Whelpton, Campbell and Patterson, 1966) found that 55 per cent of the women in its sample who had been working for 4·5 years or more were in this category. It is perhaps for this reason that this group of women (working for this length of time or more) expected fewer children than they said they wanted. There is a further distinction within those who were not subfecund and who also worked. On the one hand are those who worked because they liked working, few of whom expected more children than they wanted, and those who worked in order to supplement the family income, more of whom expected more than they wanted. The former group were clearly better planners than the latter, but of course the latter come from those socio-economic groups who are in any event characterised by less success in birth control than those in other groups. Although the authors of the study do not make the suggestion, it seems possible that for the second of these two groups, the wife's working worsens the conjugal relationship, and this could cause poorer planning success. Blake does not consider such possibilities. Several other studies document the correlation between female employment and fertility, if in less detail than the G.A.F. authors (United Nations, 1953; Freedman, Baumert and Bolte, 1958–59; Ridley, 1959).

But it is in precisely those societies for which Blake recommends the promotion of the supposed advantages of female employment that the relationship between such employment and fertility seems most erratic. The disjunction is best illustrated with data compiled and analysed by Federici (1968) for Italy. In the poor, agricultural south there is no relation between female employment and lower fertility; whereas in the north, the expected inverse relation is clearly visible. Federici has no way of separating out the subfecund wives, and is correspondingly cautious about the direction of the relationship, but suggests that even when the different mean ages of employed women in the two parts are considered, it does seem to be the case that agricultural employment is not inconsistent with 'normal' fertility in the way that secondary or tertiary employment is.

Several native analysts of conditions in the U.S.S.R. have attributed low fertility there to working women (Davtyan, 1967; Sadvokasova, 1967; Urlanis, 1967), and Szabady (1966) has suggested a similar relationship in Eastern Europe. All, however, distinguish between urban areas, where the association is clear, and rural areas where it is much less so. Even the urban relationship, however, has been challenged by Mazur (1968). He can see no association between the proportion of women working and fertility in urban areas, and but a negligible one in rural ones. It is, of course, certainly true that Soviet workers wish to explain away what is to them the embarrassment of low marital fertility and natural that they should do so by relating it to the considerable advantages that women have in a socialist society, but since their findings correspond to those in other societies, and since I can find no convincing criteria to distinguish their findings from Mazur's, it would seem, even if for this reason alone, that they should have the benefit of the doubt.

Stycos and Weller (1967) have tackled the incongruity between the fertility of working women in developed and developing societies, taking the association in the first as given and illustrating the second with Latin American and Turkish data, and they produce a typology resting on the hypothesis that where female work and maternal roles are compatible, there will be no reduction in fertility. They do not, however, specify the conditions under which such compatibility might or might not occur. Thrown back again to the patterns presented by the data (of which Federici's is typical), one can only suggest that female employment in agriculture occurs in the social organisation of the extended family in which there is, first, a greater need for children as labour and a source of potential security, and second, a greater opportunity for relying upon other kin members to take care of the children while the mother is working. A good test of this hypothesis would be to take two otherwise similar groups in a society , one with an extended kin structure and one without, and examine the strength of the relationship between female employment and fertility. To my knowledge, this has not so far been done. Were the hypothesis to be tentatively confirmed, it would follow that the promotion of gainful employment among mothers in developing societies would only serve to reduce fertility when the social and economic modernisation of those societies had already got under way, thus providing conditions for reducing fertility anyway.

(d) Urbanisation, Race and Social Mobility
In general then, whatever their other effects, and—as far as fertility is concerned—particularly their effects on birth control practices, it seems clear that the educational level and religious affiliation of the couple can affect fertility intentions.

In addition, in certain parts of certain societies a wife's decision to seek gainful employment because she wishes to work (and not because she needs the extra income), can also effect tastes for children in a negative direction. These three factors, together with the others that I have already discussed in this chapter, do not exhaust those that have been suggested at some time or another to be relevant to the determination of fertility. However, it would appear that those other factors, primarily urbanisation, race, and social mobility, when found to be related to fertility intentions, are so related through mechanisms that can better be expressed in terms of the interaction between tastes, resources and costs. Such a reduction serves to provide a clearer understanding of the causes of fertility differentials and also to provide the sociology of fertility with a more parsimonious model, indisputably a double advantage in any science.

This point is most clearly seen from an inspection of the studies on the possible relation between urbanisation and fertility (see, for an older review, United Nations, 1953; and Abu-Lughod, 1963–64; Badenhorst, Unterhalter, 1961–62; Beagle, 1966; Concepcion, 1967; Duncan, 1964; 1965; Freedman, Slesinger, 1961–62; Gendell, 1967; Goldberg, 1958–59; Goldstein, Mayer, 1965; Maisco, 1965; Robinson, 1963; Sinha, 1962; Stycos, 1965; Vavra, 1962; Yaukey, 1961; Zarate, 1967a; 1967b; Zikry, 1964). Bearing in mind the difficulties that can occur in societies in which the measurement of fertility is deficient (see Robinson, 1963), all students see an inverse relationship between fertility and urbanisation. In several studies, it has been pointed out that the effect only appears after a period of urban residence (Goldberg, 1958–59), and Gendell (1967) and Zarate (1967a), in their work on Brazil and Mexico, show that urbanisation without the concomitant rise in income and educational levels has no depressing effects at all on fertility, a conclusion that fits exactly with Heer's hypothesis (see pages 75–6). The point is that an increase in resources and/or tastes is a function of the economic and social organisation characteristic more of towns and cities than of the country, and that changes in fertility can thus be understood in terms of the models that I have already discussed.

The point is only a little less clear with the question of race.

A moment's reflection reveals that the only way in which the biological attribute of racial type could conceivably affect fertility is through fecundity, and to my knowledge fecundity, as distinct from fecundability (see Bourgeois–Pichat, 1965a), does not vary between racial types. But it is equally obvious that in so far as different races in one society occupy different social situations, whether or not the difference is an effect of their race (as it is socially defined), so their fertility is likely to vary. Consider the work of Hutchinson (1965) on white, brown and black couples in Rio de Janeiro, and Goldschneider's (1965; 1965–66; 1967) on Jewish fertility in the United States and other advanced societies.

Hutchinson's case is that racial distinctions are not independently meaningful in a causal analysis of differential fertility. He finds that although the highest proportion ever married and the highest proportion in the older age-groups occur among whites, their fertility is lowest. Mulattos have the highest fertility, and Negroes follow them closely. But there is an inverse relation with social status. Higher-status mulattos have a lower fertility than high-status whites, but of course there are fewer high-status mulattos, which serves to raise their mean fertility as a colour category. Moreover, he finds that an examination of the mobility of the 2,425 women in the sample, on the assumption that their fertility will be the mean of their class of origin and their class of destination (see the discussion of Duncan's work on mobility, below, for an elaboration and examination of this hypothesis) shows that fertility differentials can almost entirely be accounted for by the assumed hypothesis. What, he rightly asks, remains of the thesis of racial differences in fertility?

Goldschneider (1965; 1967) sampled 25 per cent of the Jewish population of Providence, R.I. in 1963, and has argued that his data are consistent with earlier, scattered studies and can be generalised with them to provide a picture of the pattern and explanations of Jewish fertility in the United States. Freedman, Whelpton and Smit (1961) had accounted for Jewish fertility in the following way:

The fertility norms and behaviour of the Jews appear to be consistent with their distinctive social and economic

8

characteristics. They have fertility characteristics we would expect to be associated with their high educational, occupational and income status, their high concentration in metropolitan areas and the small amount of farm background in their recent history. These social and economic characteristics have been associated generally in both theoretical discussions and in empirical work with low fertility, low fertility values and high rationality in family planning.

In short, there was no suggestion that being Jewish, as distinct from being a particular type of American, affected fertility in any way. Unfortunately for these authors, the Princeton Study report published in the same year (see also Westoff *et al.*, 1963) found no class differences between Jews in the sample, a fact that distinguished them from other religious groups. Goldschneider argues that Jewish fertility has differed from that to comparable Americans, and that this difference can be accounted for in terms of their acculturation to the society after immigration from Europe. For example, it was evident from early studies that the fertility of native-born Jews was lower than that for the foreign-born, and indeed whereas native white fertility dropped by 15 per cent in the period 1920–40 (following the restrictions imposed upon immigration by the United States government), that of Jews dropped by 37 per cent. Goldschneider attributes this to the efforts of second-generation immigrants to consolidate and improve their social position, a thesis he reinforces by pointing to the upswing in fertility in the third generation. The data supporting this thesis are not conclusive. The number of Jews in the Princeton sample was small, and the class differences in desired family size are little smaller than those somewhat mysteriously found for other religious. And the historical data suffer from being fragmentary and not being sufficiently detailed to permit cross-tabulations by socio-economic characteristics. At best, Goldschneider's thesis can be taken to be not inconsistent with his own data, and Freedman, Whelpton and Smit's thesis to be inconsistent only with that in the Princeton Study. Either way, there is nothing intrinsically *racial* in the explanation.

If Goldschneider's thesis is correct, the explanation for the changes in American Jewish fertility would appear to be a special case of the famous social mobility hypothesis: namely, that upward social mobility induces lower fertility intentions (see the discussion of this in Eversley, 1959; United Nations, 1953; Westoff *et al.*, 1961), The second-generation Jews would exhibit this pattern most markedly, and the higher fertility of the third generation would thus be explained as the result of a slackening in the efforts for and so rate of upward mobility. Oddly, for so attractive and neat an hypothesis, there are only two good tests of it (Berent, 1951–52; Blau, Duncan, 1967). Other studies (for instance, Westoff *et al.*, 1961; 1963; Szabady *et al.*, 1964) attempting to examine the problem have done so from data gathered primarily for other purposes. Westoff and his co-workers were particularly disappointed not to find a stronger negative association between upward mobility and fertility than they did, and suggest that one reason may have been their exclusion of the childless and the one-child families from their sample. Interestingly in the present context, they find the hypothesis supported most strongly among their Jewish sub-sample. Berent, using data gathered in the course of the London social mobility survey in 1949, and Blau and Duncan, using data gathered in conjunction with the U.S. Bureau of the census Current Population Survey in 1962, did, however, all find the expected association. Berent's conclusion was simple: upward mobility leads to lower fertility, and downward mobility to higher fertility, whether the mobility is inter- or intra-generational. Duncan (1966) has re-interpreted this data to show that the distributions can be explained by the more parsimonious hypothesis that the fertility of a couple can be explained as the additive effect of the fertility of its class of origin and its class of destination. There is no need to postulate a separate *mobility* effect at all. Blau and Duncan's own American data also fits this model, with the small proviso that downward mobility over three or more socio-economic classes increases fertility to an extent marginally greater than could have been predicted from the additive model.[10] This elegant conclusion

[10]Blau and Duncan also test, and refute, the hypothesis that *all* differential fertility can be accounted for in terms of differential mobility.

(apart from the observation on the very downwardly mobile) dismisses anything that may be called a separate mobility effect. The explanation for the fertility of the mobile can rather be accounted for in terms of the resources, aspirations and costs available to and perceived by these couples: in short, in terms of the factors that have been found to explain the fertility of the non-mobile. It may, of course, be that certain particular combinations of resources and aspirations will only occur *under conditions of* mobility, but the explanation of the resultant fertility will still have to be in terms of these factors.

8   SUMMARY

There are, therefore, two simple conclusions to this brief review of the established social determinants of fertility. The first is that several social and economic factors can affect what Davis and Blake have called the 'intervening variables' so as to increase or depress fertility. The second is that such factors can also serve to affect fertility intentions, and that they do so by altering the balance of resources, costs and tastes available to and perceived by the couple. The three-factor explanatory model enables one at one and the same time to collapse the often bewildering array of supposedly independent variables ranged in no particular logical order against fertility variables into a meaningful order so that considerable parsimony in explanation is achieved. However, as I said in elaborating the model in Chapter IV, to say simply that 'fertility can be explained by the interaction of resources, tastes and costs . . .' is not to state a testable theory; it is, rather, to specify what variables a theory must contain. It is only when specific values are attached to each variable (including fertility itself) that a testable and potentially explanatory theory can emerge.

I would not, however, claim that such relatively pious prescriptions themselves represent a successful navigation between the dual hazards of vacuity and triviality, the course that I set myself in Chapter I. To merely state the model in its most general form is to open oneself to charges of vacuity; and to specify causal connections between particular reasons and particular behaviours is perhaps to open oneself to charges of triviality. Yet, as I suggested in the theoretical argument in

Chapter IV, it may well be that we cannot construct general causal laws in the stronger sense of 'general' by looking at the effect reasons have on behaviour. The laws may only be confirmed by one instance because they are only applicable to that one instance. Whether or not we describe that instance as 'unique' seems to me a matter for our own conceptualisation. My own inclination is to concentrate more on the so-called unique, to conceptualise phenomena so that we can be exact rather than general in our descriptions, but I do not find this easy to justify. If pressed to do so, however, I would offer two arguments. First, it can reasonably be maintained that sociologists are emerging from the stage of intellectual development in which they are primarily concerned to establish a paradigm, and are now moving towards showing in detail how the insights of that paradigm can generate precise explanations of particular aspects of belief and behaviour. The paradigm will stand or fall on these explanations. Secondly, relatively vacuous generalisations will not be a sufficiently useful guide to those practical persons charged with doing something about fertility in societies in which it is a threatening social and economic problem. Both these arguments, and especially the first, need elaborating, and this I shall attempt in Chapter VI.

CHAPTER VI

Conclusion

1 EXPLANATIONS BY NORMS

'Close historical investigation of a given specialty at a given time discloses a set of recurrent and quasi-standard illustrations of various theories in their conceptual, observational and instrumental applications. These are the community's paradigms, revealed in its textbooks, lectures and laboratory exercises' (Kuhn, 1962). 'One of the fundamental principles of sociology is that when many members of a society face a recurrent common problem with important social consequences they tend to develop a normative solution for it. This solution, a set of rules for behaviour in a particular situation, becomes part of the culture, and the society indoctrinates its members to conform more or less closely to the norms by implicit or explicit rewards and punishments' (Ronald Freedman, 1963). Locked away in that 'one principle' of sociology is, I think, its paradigm: the conviction that there exists a level of social reality on a plane different from any directly observable in any one individual and which has an important causal influence on the beliefs and behaviour of individuals as well as on other social entities. The juxtaposition of Kuhn's definition and Freedman's statement of principle reveals, of course, the reflexive difficulty that sociology is immediately faced with, trying as it does to explain paradigms with paradigms. Whose paradigms are used to account for behaviour? Secondly, most sociologists would agree that while the conceptual distinctiveness of sociology is relatively clear and agreed, there is no such clarity and agreement about observational and instrumental rules. The paradigm, by comparison with those in other sciences, is not yet worked through. It is still difficult to point to a body of work that sociologists would all agree to be representative of what Kuhn would call 'normal sociological science', work carried on within the paradigm. Nevertheless, I think that Kuhn's notion is a useful one and does, with these reservations, enable one to describe economically and intelligibly what sociologists are up to.

In this chapter, I want to broaden the discussion that I began in Chapter IV and argue that the kind of model which I proposed there can resolve some of the dilemmas that still attach to the paradigm and place it on a firmer observational footing. In so doing, I shall conclude, it presents itself as a good candidate for transforming sociology from a persuasive but inconclusive perspective into a workable set of scientific rules for explaining some aspects of behaviour.

The overriding dilemma of the sociological paradigm is that its distinctiveness is almost exactly in inverse proportion to its applicability through a set of observational rules. More simply, sociology's distinctive claim is to observe and explain social properties, but in most cases these social properties are not directly observable. They are conceptual convictions that we construct from our observations of the belief and behaviour of individuals and sets of individuals. This contention, of course, does not go unchallenged. A recent argument against methodological individualism has asserted, but not argued, that 'if this theory means that in the social world only individuals are observable, it is evidently false' (Lukes, 1968). As an example of a directly observable social phenomenon, Lukes gives the procedure of a court. I am not persuaded that one is directly observing such procedures; rather, one is watching the interaction of counsel, defendant, judge and perhaps jury—individuals or groups of individuals—and *combining* those observations into the (very useful) conceptual shorthand of 'a court procedure'. Descriptions of the properties of that procedure are combinations of indicators derived from observing individuals. This may seem hair-splitting, and I certainly do not want to advocate the position of those whom Stinchcombe (1968), for example, lampoons: those who 'raise their lack of sociological intuition to the philosophical principle that only individual behaviour and motives are real'. To do that would betray an extremely primitive understanding of the nature and process of scientific conceptualisation. On the other hand, the familiar kind of sociological

'analysis', well-instanced, I think in the statement of Freedman's that I quoted earlier, raises crucial questions that cannot honestly be avoided by mere expressions of ontological
faith. McHugh (1968) puts some of these questions well.
'Norms establish the ground rules, and a social system is
stable when these norms are effective in governing interaction.
The question here is, what are the *actual* ways in which members go about their ends and means? What does an action
look like with regard to the *concrete observables* that would
describe for us the activity proposed as rule-governed? . . .
How are norms invoked during interaction, what does obeying
a rule look like concretely? Does it come out universalism
just like that, ensconced in abstraction? In what sense can
norms be said to "appear"?'[1] These are fair questions as much
to Lukes' court procedure as to McHugh's own target, Parsons
on norms in *The Structure of Social Action*. In short then, I do
not wish to impugn sociological conceptualisation; I merely
wish to make clear what is implied for observation in holding
to it.

So far, I have described the sociological paradigm, or one
view of it, in convenient shorthand. I have said that sociologists are out to explain behaviour in terms of norms. In
fact, of course, there is an array of norm-like concepts, the most
familiar of which are, besides 'norm' itself, 'rules', 'values'
and 'goals'. Rules, I think, can be taken to be synonomous
with norms. Values and goals are of a different logical order,
and distinguished between themselves by the former being
more general than the latter.[2]

Norms are prescriptions. However they are defined situ-
ationally, as ego's obligations, alter's expectations or whatever,
they always have the logical form of an 'ought' sentence. This
is their defining characteristic. It is also sometimes said,
especially by those in the Wittgensteinian and ethnomethodo-
logical schools, that norms 'define' social situations (see, e.g.,
McHugh, 1968). This can be confusing, and I think that it is
preferable to distinguish the defining function of the concepts

---

[1]The emphases are McHugh's.

[2]I take these distinctions from my own understanding of the drift of sociological
discussion. A useful summary, taking the notions of value and goal (but not norm)
apart and examining their utility for explaining fertility, is Spengler (1966).

that norms contain from the norms themselves (see Chapter IV and esp. Winch, 1958). Neither values nor goals are of this logical form. If I say that Indian fathers value sons, I am not also necessarily saying that there is a norm that Indian fathers *ought to* value sons. That may be the case, but it is a contingent matter. I think that it is sensible to distinguish between values and goals, as I have said, simply on grounds of generality. Indian fathers value sons (value); Indian fathers aim for two surviving sons (goal).

Having now, I hope, made these elementary distinctions clear, I can re-introduce the notion of 'tastes' that, following Easterlin (1969), I mentioned in Chapter IV. Easterlin himself says, in an aside and without further explanation, that norms are 'the conceptual embodiment of preferences (tastes)'. This is misleading. A taste or preference in economic analysis, like a want in some variants of political analysis (e.g. Barry, 1965), is just what it says: an expression of desire for something. Logically, then, values, goals, and tastes are of the same form. If we find that 80 per cent of Indian fathers express a taste or a preference for two sons, we may indeed say that there is a *norm* that two surviving sons are desirable in Indian society. But that is to use the notion of norm in a more trivial, statistical sense. We can, and given the chaos of confusion that can arise if we do not, probably should re-name such norms tendencies. A norm in the strong sense, the sense in which I wish to use it, is a prescription present in the society and recognised (if not necessarily accepted) by at least some members of that society.

Having made these definitions, I can return to McHugh's questions, to the problem of values, goals, tastes and norms on the ground. How do we get at them? That is not difficult, for we ask people. And that is precisely the observational point. We must, in all senses of that injunction, find them in individuals. Whether or not we go on to talk about *social* values, or norms, will depend on the proportion of individuals in a population that we find subscribing to them. The conceptual shorthand of sociology should not lead us to believe that these things exist anywhere else but in the minds of individuals. They may exist in explicit statements; they may be reconstructed from relatively inarticulate and logically incomplete utterances; or, with the greatest possible care, they may be inferred from behaviour, so long as we do not proceed to use such inferences in turn to explain the behaviour from which they have been made.

A final problem is that of the terms we use to describe the vaules, goals, tastes and norms. As I said earlier, social scientists are faced with the problem of having a paradigm for understanding paradigms. The 'community' that Kuhn refers to can be both a scientific community, which he intends, or a community of non-scientific persons. The most sensible solution to the dilemma posed by Winch, among others, which frightens so many sociologists, namely whether or not one should use the actor's own descriptions, must, I think, be a practical one. We must ask ourselves how much information loss we are prepared to tolerate. If we cannot bear to tolerate any, then we must use the actor's own description. The price we pay for this, as Davidson (1963) hints in his paper, is that we may not be able to find more than one instance of a particular description, and may not therefore be able to make any generalisations at all. On the other hand, if we want generalisations, then we must sacrifice some information for the sake of generalisable concept, a concept that will include the subtly varying descriptions given by a set of actors. Consider, for example, Duesenberry's notion (1960) of quality *versus* quantity in family size preferences. We might want to say that middle-class Americans want quality children and that Indian peasants want quantity. To say that about those Americans means conflating a whole host of particular reasons, embodying a whole range of values and goals, for having fewer rather than more children. Do we want the generalisation, or do we want the particularity? That can only be decided by each investigator according to his analytical purposes.

It is an irony that the sociology which comes from a patently unintegrated, unstable, centrifugal society, the United States, has always emphasised common values and normative consensus. Duesenberry put it well when he said that 'economics is all about how people make choices; sociology is all about how they don't have any choices to make'. In any society there is of course a variety of more or less inconsistent values, goals, tastes and norms, and in all societies actors therefore make more or less conscious choices all the time. Since most of our present sociological assumptions come from the United States, this has tended to be forgotten when it is of course glaringly problematic. The kind of model that I introduced (following Easterlin) in Chapter IV enables one to cope with choice. Sociologists, however, may feel that there are two objections to it: that it is too narrowly economic, and that is pre-supposes rationality. To the first, it may be replied that the concept of 'resources' need not only refer to income and wealth; there are also the scarce resources of time, energy and ability to assess logically varying ends and realise an optimal solution through the implementation of the most appropriate means. We all run out of these resources at some point: what is empirically interesting is our threshold on each and its implications for the choices we make. Further, and in reply to the second objection, these choices need not be rational in any strong sense. All that the model demands is that the actor it is applied to will have at least one preference, and that he or she does not have unlimited resources to realise it. This demand probably defines, indeed, the necessary conditions for regarding someone as a human agent at all. A person with no preferences and aware of no resource constraint would only be a pathetic vegetable in a mental hospital. Nothing else in the model is assumed; everything else is a matter for empirical investigation.

2 EXPLANATIONS OF NORMS

In general, and certainly in the area of the social determinants of fertility, sociologists deal with values and norms as causal factors rather than as *explicanda*. In his characterisation of the sociological paradigm, Freedman suggests that norms (and, by implication, values too) are generated from a common confrontation with some recurrent social problem. In itself, this is not particularly illuminating, and it is an issue rarely examined by sociologists. I feel that one of the best discussions is still that by Rousseau (1755). The kind of model that one needs, as he saw, must contain three elements: first, an understanding of the conceptual capacities of men; second, a delineation of the values and norms before the change; and third, an understanding of how a situational exigency effects a re-arrangement of the existing values and norms into a new conceptual pattern. Sociologists pay extraordinarily little attention to the first of these, yet current advances in psychology, linguistics and even in anthropology are suggesting that such capacities may be empirically determined and, further, that they may place constraints upon the kinds of mental and social arrangements that an individual can conceive of and put into effect. For too long, the assumption in sociology has been that, as individuals, men are rather as Locke imagined them: *tabulae rasae* upon which the 'social environment' imprints its patterns. The intellectual revolution that followed Vico through Rousseau into Kant and Marx and modern psychology and linguistics might never have happened.

The second element in this extremely simple model needs no elaboration. It presents no conceptual or practical problems that I have not considered above. Since I do not think that I have anything very useful to say about the first, I shall restrict myself to the third.

By 'situational exigency' I mean the kind of thing Durkheim was talking about in *The Division of Labour in Society*, and which is gradually re-appearing in one or two places after the hegemonic half-century of normative determinism in sociology (e.g. Lockridge, 1968; Stevenson, 1968). This is a pressing ecological (environmental, economic, political) problem which either forces a conscious re-ordering of the pre-existing values and norms into a new combination (a mechanism outlined in Lévi–Strauss, 1955: 182), or works through unconscious or semi-conscious mechanisms to affect norms or certain (psychological and physiological) resources. Durkheim, it will be remembered, discussed (albeit very briefly) a mechanism working through from the 'material density' of a society to its 'dynamic density' and so to the normative structure. It is essentially a reformulation of Rousseau's second *Discourse*. Lockridge examines the effect of rising population density under conditions of pressing land-shortage in seventeenth- and eighteenth-century New England and its effects on stratification and power relationships. Stevenson takes issue with an old statement of Evans–Pritchard and Fortes to the effect that population density in Africa has no discernible causal influence on the extent to which state-like political structures emerge.

The first of the two mechanisms by which such exigencies can affect behaviour is very familiar. Easterlin's (1962; 1966) discussion of the changing constraints of household income on fertility behaviour in the United States (see Chapter IV) is an excellent example. The second mechanism, however, is perhaps less obvious. I said earlier that some of the resources to be taken into account under that heading in the model that I was proposing were energy and the ability to assess logically varying ends and realise an optimal solution through the implementation of the most appropriate means. These psychological facilities will clearly be affected by situational exigencies of varying stress. Also, and especially in the area of fertility, it is almost certain that maternal psychological stress can have some effect on fecundity and the ability to bring a conception to term (see, for example, Stott, 1962; James, 1969): have, that is, physiological effects.

3 SUMMARY

That completes my examination of the sociological, as distinct from the social, implications of my model. I have not, be it noted, made any new theoretical points. I have merely tried to face sociologists who talk in general terms about 'normative factors' and so forth up to their analytical responsibilities. As I made clear in Chapter IV and repeated at the end of Chapter V, it is possible that the kinds of causal generalisation that any model including reasons as explanatory factors can produce will be very limited in scope. I do not think that this is particularly important. What *is* important is that we have a coherent and precise understanding of the causal mechanisms in the determination of fertility. Social causes are very important, although not by any means exclusively so, and a coherent and precise understanding of how they work is a *sine qua non* of useful advice to those involved in trying to ameliorate the population problem in afflicted countries.

APPENDIX

COMPONENTS OF NATURAL FERTILITY

Two concepts dominate the discussions of natural fertility. The first is fecundability, the probability of conceiving within one menstrual cycle; and the second, foetal death. The two are sometimes combined into a measure of *effective*, as distinct from *gross*, fecundability. These measures refer to the performance of individual women, and the calculated probabilities can, of course, be aggregated for any population whose relevant parameters are known. Before doing this, however, the proportion of sterile women must be found.

A measure of sterility inferred from fertility will not be able to distinguish precisely between male and female sterility, except in so far as over-time comparisons are possible of sterility rates within one population, where the increase in sterility from t_1 to t_2 can be attributed to female sterility on the assumption that whereas female sterility increases with age, male sterility does not. Figures therefore refer to married women, but the figures ascribed to them are in fact the sterility of the couples of which they form one half. Vincent and Henry at the Institut National d'Études Demographiques have together developed an intricate method for calculating age-specific sterility rates on modern populations and a more simple one for use on historical populations. They discuss these in a series of papers (Vincent, 1961; Henry, 1953a; 1953b; 1965a). Henry arrived at the following results (Table A-I). The first row refers to women married in England and Wales at the middle of the last century; the second to rural Japan at about 1925; and the third presents the means of five series of percentages of sterile women by age, the five series referring respectively to French–Canadians at the beginning of the eighteenth century, the 1550–1650 generations of the Genevan bourgeoisie, the inhabitants of Crulai (Normandy) at the end of the seventeenth and the beginning of the eighteenth century, three parishes in the Ile-de-France between 1740 and 1802, and Europeans in nineteenth-century Tunis.

TABLE A-I

		Age in Years				
		20	25	30	35	40
England	..	4	7·5	13	21	36
Japan ..	..	5	12·5	23	38·5	61
Others	..	3*	5	8	15	32*

Source: Henry (1965a).
*Four series rather than five.

These age-specific sterility rates must not be taken entirely at their face value. Henry is forced to assume that the populations involved are not practising birth control, but unfortunately (for the purposes of the calculations) this assumption can never be proven. At best, the figures refer to populations in which the practice of birth control was very scarce indeed if not entirely absent. The dangers of taking any historical population without further investigation, even if that population predates the introduction of mechanical methods of contraception and there is no recorded abortion or infanticide, are evident from the fertility rates that Wrigley (1966a) has reconstructed for seventeenth century Colyton in Devon. For Crulai, Henry has also calculated a more sophisticated statistic, which he calls the 'terminal fertility' rate, and which takes mortality into account. This is more satisfactory than the sterility rate, but also, of course, more difficult to calculate. These are his results (Table A-II):

TABLE A-II

	Age in Years					
	20	25	30	35	40	45
Terminal Infertility	0*	2·5–5*	11–12	20·5	54–55	97
Sterility	2	3	7	15	36	—

Source: Henry (1965a); Gautier, Henry (1958).
*These two numbers should, theoretically, be larger than those in the row below, but have been subject to errors resulting from being calculated on a small base.

Above, I said that before investigating the fecundability of married women in a population one had to determine the proportion among them that were sterile. Unfortunately, the two states are not clearly distinct. First, since fecundability drops fairly steadily after thirty-five to the menopause at about fifty, any measure of sterility within these ages will be contaminated by a hidden measure of such a drop. And second, it is not clear that all childless women are sterile in the biological sense. Stallworthy (reported in Clark, 1967) and James (1964–65) have discussed this possibility. In view of these difficulties, 'sterility' must be understood in this context as a strictly statistical, rather than biological, concept (Henry, 1965a). Nevertheless, isolating apparently sterile women in the way that I have described does make fecundability estimates more reliable.

These estimates consist mostly of inferences made from observed conception delays in populations believed not to have practised or to be practising any deliberate control, whether by contraception, abortion or infanticide before the birth is recorded. Much of the work has been done on historical French populations (including the marriage cohorts of the 1920s, a period in which French fertility was so low that the government of the day established a prize fund to restore it, thus encouraging couples to maximise their fecundity). Most American work has been done from observations on the Hutterites, an anabaptist group settled in the north-western United States and the prairie provinces of Canada (Eaton, Mayer, 1953; Tietze, 1957; Sheps, 1965–66). In the Hutterite community in Dakota in 1950, Eaton and Mayer recorded a median age at marriage of twenty-two years and a median family size of 10·6 children.

Effective fecundability, or the probability of producing a live birth, and therefore birth intervals themselves (the units from which the inferences are made) are a function of gross fecundability, post-partum infecundability and foetal loss (Vincent, 1961; Potter, 1963; James, 1963–64; 1964–65; Henry, 1957; 1961a; 1961b; 1964; 1964–65; Potter, Westoff, Sagi, 1963). Gross fecundability, first, is in turn a function of the length of the fertile period and of coital frequency. Potter (1961) has suggested that the fertile period may be much shorter than previously realised, lasting perhaps for a period of between 18 and 36 hours in any menstrual cycle. There is some evidence that not all menstrual cycles contain a fertile period, thus reducing the total fertile period in any set of cycles. Potter calculated that observed fecundabilities were consistent with a coital frequency of between seven and eleven per cycle. Evidence on coital frequency to support these inferences is obviously very difficult to obtain, and where workers do not rely on Kinsey's findings (1948; 1953) for Western societies or a few scanty reports of doubtful validity and reliability from other countries (Bourgeois–Pichat, 1965a), they work on assumed frequencies which correspond most nearly to both inferred rates and the few doubtful observations. Bourgeois–Pichat, for example, uses the alternative assumptions of eight and twelve per cycle, at ages 20 to 24. Henry (1963) has commented on the fluctuations in coital rates that can be expected over the sexually active period of a couple's marriage, pointing out that they are highest immediately after marriage. They also decline with age.

The period of post-partum infecundity, associated with the puerperium and lactation that consists partly of a period of amenorrhoea, and partly of reduced or absent ovulation during the first few menstrual cycles, is probably the most significant variable in determining effective fecundability. Unfortunately, it is also a very variable variable. In the Normandy village of Crulai that Henry studied, it appeared to last for twelve months (twenty-one including the period of gestation), whereas amongst the Hutterites it may average

9

as low as 6.1 months. This variation has led to several arguments about estimates of fecundability, the most informative of which is that between James (1963–64; 1964–65) and Henry (1964–65).[1] Sheps' recent work on the Hutterites emphasises their peculiarity in this respect (1965–66). There is little evidence on why their period of infecundability should be so low. Sheps reports that it is said that Hutterite mothers continue to breast-feed their infants until another pregnancy intervenes, so that many women never menstruate between their first pregnancy and their last. 'If these statements are accurate, they suggest that lactation may affect ovulation less in this population than in others, or perhaps that they introduce supplemental feeding sooner and (that ovulation) is thus inhibited for a shorter time.'

Recent work on the third factor in effective fecundability, foetal loss, has suggested that earlier estimates of its incidence were far too low. The 1949 Report of the Royal Commission on the British population suggested a rate of 9 per cent of all pregnancies, plus 4 per cent stillbirths. Present calculations rest on the observations of Shapiro, Jones and Demsen for New York (1962) and of French and Bierman (1962) for Hawaii, the only extensive observations in the first six months of pregnancy. Records of intra-uterine mortality for the other three months are better, and reported in most standard sources of descriptive statistics. Shapiro's New York figures are given in Table A—III.

TABLE A—III

Age of mother ..	Below 20	20–24	25–29	30–34	35–39	40–44
Ratio of intra-uterine deaths to live births ..	0·357	0·258	0·323	0·495	0·672	0·873

Bourgeois–Pichat (1965a; 1965b) estimates that somewhere between 23·8 and 34·8 per cent of all pregnancies result in foetal death: that is, approximately 30 per cent. There is a great deal of circumstantial evidence to suggest that such death is most probable in the period immediately following

---

[1]Since this was written, Wolfers (1968) has criticised the assumptions made by Henry, James and Potter, and produced rather lower estimates of fecundability: see bibliographical note to his article.

conception, but this cannot be confirmed until such time as detection techniques are improved beyond their present state.

These are the factors usually considered in discussions and calculations of natural fertility. One point remains to be clarified: what proportion of the variance in family size in a population can be attributed to non-social, involuntary factors? A moment's thought will reveal that such a calculation demands very stringent demographic conditions: women of comparable age at, and duration of marriage not practising birth control in any form and who are all to some extent fecund. Bodmer and Jacquard (1968), developing the probability models suggested by Sheps (1965) and others, have performed such a calculation on the Hutterites, who meet these conditions most nearly of well-documented populations. They found that a predicted variance of 5·83 constrasted with an actual one of 13·91, and conclude that 'the difference between these two variances can be considered as a measure of the heterogeneity of the fecundity of Hutterite women'. So far, comparable calculations have not been made for modern Western populations, but it is of course clear that the greater the practice of contraception, the smaller the amount of variance that can be attributed to non-voluntary factors.

Annotated Bibliography

All works cited in the text are listed, together with a number of additional titles. The bibliography is updated to late 1968. Items published before 1962 are covered very selectively; for these, reference should also be made to FREEDMAN (1961–62). Copies of this can now be obtained from Johnson Reprints, Berkeley Square House, London W.1. or 111 Fifth Avenue, New York, N.Y. 10003. At least three essential books and several important papers have been published in the interval between writing and publication: these include BEHRMAN et al. (1969), KISER et al. (1968) and WRIGLEY (1969). With the exception of Easterlin's paper in BEHRMAN, their contents have not been incorporated into the text. I am grateful to Professors Easterlin and Ryder for advance copies of their papers in BEHRMAN. The bibliography can be kept up to date from lists published regularly in *Population* (Institut National d'Etudes Demographiques, Paris) and *Population Index* (Office of Population Research, Princeton for the Population Association of America Inc.). I would welcome notice of serious omissions.

ABU–LUGHOD, J. (1963–64). 'Urban–rural differences as a function of the demographic transition', *American Journal of Sociology* 69: 476–90. Data from 1960 census of Egypt. For other analyses of urban–rural differences, see references in text. See also ABU–LUGHOD (1965); RIZK (1963); YAUKEY (1961).

ABU–LUGHOD, J. (1965). 'The emergence of differential fertility in urban Egypt', *Milbank Memorial Fund Quarterly* 43: 235–53. Data from the 1960 census of Egypt. Finds that fertility strongly related to age at marriage and education in the expected directions; also related to occupation, but less strongly than to wife's education. The independence of the husband's occupation effect and that of the wife's education was not tested. See ABU–LUGHOD (1963–64); RIZK (1963); YAUKEY (1961).

ADELMAN, I. (1963). 'An econometric analysis of population growth', *American Economic Review* 53: 314–39. 37 countries studied from data relating to the period 1947–57 for any relationships between age-specific birth rates, real per capita income, the proportion of non-agricultural workers in the population, the level of literacy, the population density, the infant mortality rate and the rate of growth of per capita income. First four variables accounted for 50–70 per cent of the variance in the birth rate. Education was the most strongly related of the four; see HEER (1966a). See also text, and WEINTRAUB (1962); RUSSETT et al. (1964); FRIEDLANDER, SILVER (1967).

ADELMAN, I., MORRIS, C. T. (1965–66). 'A quantitative study of social and political determinants of fertility', *Economic Development and Cultural Change* 14: 129–57. See text.

AGARWALA, S. N. (1957). 'The age at marriage in India', *Population Index* 23: 96–107.

AGARWALA, S. N. (1961–62). 'A family planning survey in four Delhi villages', *Population Studies* 15: 110–20. An excellent and informative survey of levels of knowledge about family planning and methods of birth control in India, finding that knowledge increases with higher ages, thus suggesting that the motivation for contraception intensifies as parity rises. See also BERELSON (1966); MAULDIN (1965a).

AGARWALA, S. N. (1964). 'Social and cultural factors affecting fertility in India', *Population Review* (Madras) 8: 73–8. A summary; see also GUPTA, MALAKER (1963);

JAIN (1964); MAYER (1960); NAG (1967); PAKRASI, MALAKER (1967); POTTER, NEW
WYON, GORDON (1965); SINHA (1962); SAMUEL (1963); LORIMER (1967); DRIVER
(1963).

AGARWALA, S. N. (1967). 'Effect of a rise in female marriage age on birth rate in
India', *in* UNITED NATIONS DEPARTMENT OF ECONOMIC AND SOCIAL AFFAIRS: *Pro-
ceedings of the World Population Conference*, II, New York: United Nations: 172.
See text; and DAS (1967); TALWAR (1967); COALE, TYE (1961).

ANASTASI, A. (1956). 'Intelligence and family size', *Psychological Bulletin* 53: 187–209.
A review of past work. See BAJEMA (1966).

ARDENER, E. (1962). *Divorce and fertility: an African study*. London: Oxford University
Press. Field study of the Bakweri in Nigeria, finding an adverse effect of divorce
on fertility. See CARR–SAUNDERS (1922); NAG (1962).

BACCI, M. L. (1968). 'Fertility and nuptiality changes in Spain from the late 18th to
the early 20th century', *Population Studies* 22: 83–102; 211–34.

BACHI, R., MATRAS, J. (1962). 'Contraception and induced abortions among Jewish
maternity cases in Israel', *Milbank Memorial Fund Quarterly* 40: 207–29. Data
from 3000 maternity cases, 1959–60. Finds that European and American immigrants resort more to contraception and abortion than Asian and African ones.
See MATRAS, AUERBACH (1962); BACHI, MATRAS (1964).

BACHI, R., MATRAS, J. (1964). 'Family size preferences of Jewish maternity cases in
Israel', *Milbank Memorial Fund Quarterly* 42: 38–56. Sample as in BACHI, MATRAS
(1962). See that, and MATRAS, AUERBACH (1962); TALMON–GARBER (1959).

BADENHORST, L. T. (1962–63). 'Family limitation and methods of contraception in
an urban population', *Population Studies* 16: 286–301. A South African study, in
which findings are compared with those from the first GAF report; see FREED-
MAN, WHELPTON, CAMPBELL (1959).

BADENHORST, L. T., UNTERHALTER, R. (1961–62). 'A study of fertility in an urban
African community', *Population Studies* 15: 70–86. See also BADENHORST (1962–
63).

BAJEMA, C. J. (1966). 'Relation of fertility to educational attainment in a Kalamazoo
public school population: a follow-up study', *Eugenics Quarterly* 13: 306–15. Native
whites, born 1916–17, whose intelligence was measured in the sixth grade. Finds
that intermediate groups have lower fertility; no mechanism suggested, but a
methodologically very careful study.

BALTZELL, D. (1953). 'Social mobility and fertility in an elite group', *Milbank Memorial Fund Quarterly* 31: 411–20. The Philadelphia elite in 1940. 149 males in the
upper class and the 'functional elite' had a larger family size than 352 in the
functional elite only, suggesting a negative relation between mobility and fertility. Interesting in that it deals with a high-status group. For methodologically
adequate studies of mobility, see BERENT (1951–52); DUNCAN (1966); BLAU, DUN-
CAN (1967).

BANKS, J. A. (1954). *Prosperity and parenthood*. London: Routledge and Kegan Paul.
Sub-titled 'a study of family planning among the Victorian middle classes', this
is a classic. Banks attempts to reconstruct the reasoning of the English middle
classes in the 1870s that led them to cut back their fertility, and concludes that
they did so in order to maintain their standard of living. From the fact that these
groups were the first in the English population to adopt family limitation on any
scale, BANKS infers that the reasoning and the practice diffused downwards into
the working class. This inference would not appear to be justified: see CARLSSON
(1966–67). See also GENERAL REGISTER OFFICE (1917; 1923); GLASS (1938); LEWIS–
FANING (1949); PIERCE, ROWNTREE (1961–62). Several texts have, nevertheless,
adopted BANKS' thesis of diffusion: see, for example, BESHERS (1967). See also
BANKS (1968).

BANKS, J. A. (1968). 'Historical sociology and the study of population', *Proceedings of
the American Academy of Arts and Sciences* 97: 397–414. In which BANKS repeats the
diffusion thesis. See BANKS (1954).

BANKS, J. A., BANKS, O. (1964). *Feminism and family planning in Victorian England*. Liverpool: Liverpool University Press. A supplement to BANKS (1954); argues against
the effect of the feminist movement on the promotion of a positive climate for

birth control in later nineteenth-century England. For another discussion of feminist ideas and family planning, see STYCOS (1962).

BARCLAY, G. W. (1958). *Techniques of Population Analysis*. New York: Wiley. An introductory handbook.

BARRY, B. M. (1965). *Political Argument*. London: Routledge.

BATES, J. E., ZAWADZKI, E. S. (1964). *Criminal abortion: a study in medical sociology*. Springfield Ill.: Thomas. See also CALDERONE (1958); GEBHARD *et al.* (1959).

BECKER, G. S. (1960). 'An economic analysis of fertility', *in* UNIVERSITIES–NATIONAL BUREAU COMMITTEE FOR ECONOMIC RESEARCH: *Demographic and Economic Change in Developed Countries*. Princeton: Princeton University Press: 209–31. An explanation of American fertility in terms of the classical consumption model, sophisticated but paying little attention to tastes or preferences. See DUESENBERRY (1960); EASTERLIN (1969); BLAKE (1968).

BEEGLE, J. A. (1966). 'Social structure and changing fertility of the farm population', *Rural Sociology* 31: 415–27. An American study. See DUNCAN (1965); GOLDBERG (1958–59).

BEHRMAN, S. J., CORSA, L. JR., FREEDMAN, R. (eds.) (1969). *Fertility and Family Planning: a world view*. Ann Arbor: University of Michigan Press. A collection of 20 authoritative papers covering biological, social, economic and policy aspects of fertility. Particularly useful as an introduction in view of the fact that research now progresses too quickly for integrated texts. See also SHEPS, RIDLEY (1965).

BERELSON, B. (1966). 'KAP studies on fertility', *in* BERELSON, B., *et al.* (eds.): *Family Planning and Population Programmes*. Chicago and London: University of Chicago Press: 655–68. A summary discussion of surveys of knowledge, attitudes and practice on fertility in developing countries, containing a review of data on the relationship between ideal and actual family sizes. See MAULDIN (1965a).

BERELSON, B., FREEDMAN, R. (1964). 'A study in fertility control', *Scientific American* 110 (May): 29–37. A description of the intensive birth control programme in Taichung, Taiwan. See also TAUBER (1961); FREEDMAN, PEN, TAKESHITA, SUN (1963); FREEDMAN, TAKESHITA, SUN (1964); FREEDMAN (1965); TAKESHITA (1966; 1967); COLLVER, SPEARE, LIU (1966–67). For a criticism of fertility control programmes as they are at present organised, see STYCOS (1962); and for a criticism of their ends, DAVIS (1967).

BERENT, J. (1951–52). 'Fertility and social mobility', *Population Studies* 5: 244–60. See text; and DUNCAN (1966).

BERENT, J. (1953). 'The relationship between family sizes of two successive generations', *Milbank Memorial Fund Quarterly* 31: 39–50. 1949 L.S.E. social mobility data (see GLASS, D. V. (ed.): *Social Mobility in Britain*. London: Routledge and Kegan Paul, 1954). Finds a small positive association between family sizes over generations. See also DUNCAN, FREEDMAN, COBLE, SLESINGER (1965).

BERGUES, H., ARIES, P., HELIN, E., HENRY, L., RIQUET, R. P. M., SAUVY, A., SUTTER, J. (1960). *La Prévention des Naissances dans la Famille*. Paris: Presses Universitaires de France *for the* Institut National d'Études Démographiques. A thorough study of the history of birth control in French marriages since the onset of the fertility decline there at the end of the eighteenth century. SUTTER, in the section 'Sur la diffusion des méthodes contraceptives', discusses and criticises the standard diffusion thesis: see text; BANKS (1954); CARLSSON (1966–67). See also 'La limitation . . .' (1956); WEILL–HALLÉ (1967); SIEBERT, SUTTER (1964); COALE, *in* BEHRMAN (1969).

BESHERS, J. M. (1967). *Population Processes in Social Systems*. New York and London: Collier–Macmillan. A simple-minded review of the main sociological issues and their methodology in population studies. In his section on fertility, BESHERS ignores completely the work on pre-industrial and primitive populations, and indeed all vital events prior to 1800; subscribes to a naive diffusion thesis, which rests on inadequate data; and proposes a formal model of diffusion which, although elegant, is not useful since it rests on misleading premises. See BANKS (1954); CARLSSON (1966–67).

BIRABEN, J.–N. (1967). 'Prevailing fertility situation and its causes in Western Europe', *in* UNITED NATIONS DEPARTMENT OF ECONOMIC AND SOCIAL AFFAIRS:

World Population Conference 1965, II, New York: United Nations: 190–96. Foresees a consolidation of the recent pattern of decreasing variance around a mean family size. For a similar, although demographically more comprehensive, discussion of American data, see RYDER (1969). Also GLASS (1968).

BIRDSELL, J. B. (1953). 'Some environmental and cultural factors influencing the structuring of Australian aboriginal populations', *American Naturalist* 87: 169–207. Discusses the fertility regulator of infanticide through circumcision and subincision practised by these populations in times of hardship.

BLAKE, J. (1961). *Family Structure in Jamaica: the Social Context of Reproduction.* New York: Free Press. An intensive study of 99 lower class women and 53 of their mates in Jamaica. Concludes that although the motivations of both women and men in this group towards family size are contradictory, the effect of discontinuous consensual unions is to lower fertility. See also STYCOS (1964); BRAITHWAITE, ROBERTS (1961); MORTARA (1961); and for another Caribbean situation, HILL, STYCOS, BACK (1959).

BLAKE, J. (1965). 'Demographic science and the redirection of population policy', *in* SHEPS, RIDLEY (1965): 41–69. See text; also DAVIS (1967).

BLAKE, J. (1966). 'Ideal family size among white Americans: a quarter of a century's evidence', *Demography* 3: 154–73.

BLAKE, J. (1966–67). 'The Americanisation of Catholic reproductive ideals', *Population Studies* 20: 27–43. See also BLAKE (1965); (1966); (1967a); (1967b); (1967c).

BLAKE, J. (1967a). 'Income and reproductive motivation', *Population Studies* 21 185–206. See text; and BLAKE (1968).

BLAKE–DAVIS, J. (1967b). 'Parental control, delayed marriage and population policy', *in* UNITED NATIONS DEPARTMENT OF ECONOMIC AND SOCIAL AFFAIRS: *World Population Conference*, II, New York: United Nations: 132–36.

BLAKE, J. (1967c). 'Reproductive ideals and educational attainment among white Americans, 1943–66', *Population Studies* 21: See BLAKE (1966).

BLAKE, J. (1968). 'Are babies consumer durables? A critique of the economic theory of reproductive motivation', *Population Studies* 22: 5–25. A criticism particularly of BECKER (1960). However, as EASTERLIN (1969) points out with reference to another of BLAKE's papers, she misunderstands the nature of the utility argument in so far as it makes 'tastes' a variable. This variable is conceptually equivalent to her 'institutional prescriptions' and, as EASTERLIN again emphasises, has the virtue of making fertility decisions intelligible within one model. BLAKE is nevertheless effectively critical of BECKER's own evidence for the hypothesis that under conditions of universal contraceptive effectiveness, fertility will be directly related to income. See BECKER (1960); EASTERLIN (1969).

BLAU, P. M. (1964). *Exchange and Power in Social Life.* New York and London: Wiley. A recent statement of exchange theory in sociology, working from the assumption that social relationships rest on the maximisiation of certain utilities. Unfortunately, logically ambiguous, wavering between deductive and developmental arguments. See HEATH (1968).

BLAU, P. M., DUNCAN, O. D. (1967). *The American Occupational Structure.* New York: Wiley. Pp. 361–99 report on an analysis of differential fertility and occupational mobility in a sub-sample (c.6,000) of the main sample, characterised by the wives having finished the period of childbearing by March 1962. With BERENT (1951–52), re-analysed by DUNCAN (1966), the best source on fertility and mobility.

BLAYO, C. (1968). 'Fécondité des mariages de 1946 à 1964 en France', *Population* 23: 649–738.

BODMER, W. F., JACQUARD, A. (1968). 'La variance de la dimension des familles, selon divers facteurs de la fécondité', *Population* 23: 869–78. Calculates that half of the variance in fertility under constant demographic conditions in Hutterites due to differential fecundity. See EATON, MAYER (1953) and other references at that entry.

BOGUE, D. J. (ed.) (1967). *Sociological Contributions to Family Planning Research.* Chicaog: University of Chicago Press. A useful collection of papers. See also BERELSON (1966); KISER (1962); SHEPS, RIDLEY (1965); OHLIN (1967); MURAMATSU, HARPER (1966); BEHRMAN (1969).

BOGUE, D. J. (1969). *Principles of Demography*, New York and London: Wiley. Recent and thorough. Section on 'human natality' contains much recent American data; for similar data, see also KISER, GRABILL, CAMPBELL (1968).

BOURGEOIS–PICHAT, J. (1965a). 'Les facteurs de la fécondité non dirigée', *Population* 20: 383–424.

BOURGEOIS–PICHAT, J. (1965b). 'Relation between foetal-infant mortality and fertility', *in* UNITED NATIONS DEPARTMENT OF ECONOMIC AND SOCIAL AFFAIRS: *Proceedings of the World Population Conference*, II, New York: United Nations: 68–72. 1965a elaborates a typology of 280 possible types of natural fertility; 1965b discusses in detail the a_L type described in the text. 1965a is the best general source on natural fertility.

BRACKETT, J. W. (1962). 'Demographic trends and population policy in the Soviet Union', *in* JOINT ECONOMIC COMMITTEE, CONGRESS OF THE UNITED STATES: *Dimensions of Soviet Economic Power*.Washington: Government Printing Office: 487–589: See also PETERSEN (1961); HEER (1968); LORIMER (1946).

BRADSHAW, B. S. (1969). 'Fertility differences in Peru: a reconsideration', *Population Studies* 23: 5–19. In context of debate (see text Ch. V; HEER, 1964–65; HEER, TURNER 1964–65; JAMES, 1966–67; HEER, 1967; WHITEHEAD, 1968) shows that Indian fertility equal to or possibly higher than Spanish.

BRAITHWAITE, L., ROBERTS, G. W. (1960–61). 'A gross mating table for a West Indian population', *Population Studies* 14: 198–217. See also BLAKE (1961); MORTARA (1961); STYCOS (1964); and for Puerto Rico, HILL, STYCOS, BACK (1959).

BREZNIK, D. (1968). 'Fertility of the Yugoslav population', *in* SZABADY, E. (ed.) *World Views of Population Problems*, Budapest: Akadémiai Kaidó: 53–67. Recent data, analysed into differentials by urban-rural area and nationality.

BURCH, T. K. (1966). 'The fertility of American Catholics: a comparative overview', *Demography* 3: 174–87. See also WESTOFF, *et al.* (1961; 1963); FREEDMAN, WHELPTON, CAMPBELL (1959); WHELPTON, CAMPBELL, PATTERSON (1966). And for a test of Burch's findings against French-Canadian data, KROTKI, LAPIERRE (1968).

CALDERONE, M. S. (ed.) (1958). *Abortion in the United States*. New York: Hoeber. Papers given at a Planned Parenthood Federation conference (New York, 1955). See also BATES, ZAWADZKI (1964); GEBHARD *et al.* (1959); TIETZE (1965a; 1965b). To this writer's knowledge, no new data have appeared to contradict or qualify the estimate of between 200,000 and 1,200,000 abortions a year in the U.S.A. that appears in this book. For Great Britain, see FAMILY PLANNING ASSOCIATION (1966).

CALDWELL, J. C. (1967). 'Fertility differentials as evidence of incipient fertility decline in a developing country: the case of Ghana', *Population Studies* 21: 23–32. See also DEMENY *et al.* (1968b); CALDWELL *in* BERELSON (1966).

CAMPBELL, A. A. (1967). 'Recent fertility trends in the United States and Canada', *in* UNITED NATIONS DEPARTMENT OF ECONOMIC AND SOCIAL AFFAIRS: *World Population Conference 1965*, II, New York: United Nations: 200–04. Expresses the conviction that the shift away from childless and one-child families 'must be related to some equally impressive changes in our culture, and (that) these changes may well be economic in nature even though they are not measured by the commonly used indexes of economic conditions; . . . (but that) there is as yet no evidence that the total number of children that couples have is influenced by economic conditions *per se*'. Campbell, at the Scripps Foundation, is currently investigating the relationship between family building and economic conditions. See EASTERLIN (1962; 1966; 1969); FREEDMAN, COOMBS (1966b); BLAKE (1967); KISER *et al.* (1969).

CARISSE, C. (1964). *Planification des naissances en milieu Canadian-Français*. Montreal: Presses de l'Université de Montreal. The modern situation in a population traditionally characterised by high fertility; for the historical situation, see HENRIPIN (1954).

CARLETON, R. O. (1965). 'Labour force participation: a stimulus to fertility in Puerto Rico?', *Demography* 2: 233–39. Data (1960) on children born to married women in San Juan Standard Metropolitan Area. Finds a *positive* relation between wife's education, wife's working and fertility. No comparisons over time possible.

CARLSSON, G. (1966–67). 'The decline of fertility: innovation or adjustment process',

Population Studies 20: 149–74. A very important article, challenging the more simple-minded conventional wisdom of the diffusion thesis of contraception and fertility decline. Presents differential regional data from Sweden, 1860–1946. See text.

CARR–SAUNDERS, A. (1922). *The Population Problem*. Oxford: Clarendon Press. The classic statement of the theory that populations are regulated at an optimum level for their resources, illustrated from anthropological data. See WYNNE–EDWARDS (1962).

CHO, L. J. (1964). 'Estimated refined measures of fertility for all major countries of the world', *Demography* 1: 359–74.

CHO, L.–J., GRABILL, W. H., BOGUE, D. J. (in preparation): *Differential Fertility of the American Population*.

CHOU, R.–C., BROWN, S. (1968). 'A comparison of the size of families of Roman Catholics and non-Catholics in Great Britain', *Population Studies* 22: 51–60. 1966 Gallup data on 263 Catholic and 263 non-Catholic married men in England, Wales and Scotland. See text; and for American summaries, BLAKE (1966–67), BURCH (1966).

CHOW, LIEN–PIN, FREEDMAN, R., POTTER, R. G., JAIN, A. K. (1968). 'Correlates of I.U.D. termination in a mass family planning programme', *Milbank Memorial Fund Quarterly* 46 (2, pt. 1): 215–35. Taiwan.

CLARK, C. (1967). *Population Growth and Land Use*. London: Macmillan. A poorly-argued case for the economic and social benefits of rising populations, incidentally including a summary of much evidence on natural and differential fertility.

COALE, A. J. (1965). 'Birth rates, death rates, and rates of growth in human population', *in* SHEPS, RIDLEY, (1965): 242–65. A clear but technical discussion of the formal demography of population change. Includes an examination of the stable population theory. See BARCLAY (1958); COX (1966); and LOTKA (1925).

COALE, A. J. (1967). 'Factors associated with the development of low fertility: an historic summary', *in* UNITED NATIONS DEPARTMENT OF ECONOMIC AND SOCIAL AFFAIRS: *World Population Conference* 1965, II, New York: United Nations: 205–09. A short, lucid and illuminating account of the relative contribution of the proportion married and birth control within marriage to the fertility decline in the West (and the industrialised East). This contribution can be expressed in the formula:

$I_f = I_g I_m + (1 - I_m) I_h$, where:

f_i	. . .	births per woman in $_i$th age interval
g_i	. . .	births per married woman in $_i$th age interval
h_i	. . .	births per non-married woman in $_i$th age interval
w_i	. . .	number of women in $_i$th age interval
m_i	. . .	number of married women in $_i$th age interval
u_i	. . .	number of non-married women in $_i$th age interval
F_i	. . .	births per woman in the $_i$th age interval in the standard population, married Hutterites 1921–30
I_f	. . .	$\Sigma f_i w_i / \Sigma F_i w_i$ the index of overall fertility
I_g	. . .	$\Sigma g_i m_i / \Sigma F_i m_i$ the index of fertility of married women
I_h	. . .	$\Sigma h_i u_i / \Sigma F_i u_i$ the index of fertility of non-married women
I_m	. . .	$\Sigma F_i m_i / F_i w_i$ the index of the proportion married.

See text; and, for work carried out within this framework, DEMENY (1968a); VAN DE WALLE (1968); also, for a similar approach, MATRAS (1965a; 1965b; 1965–66).

COALE, A. J., FALLERS, L. A., LEVY, M. J. JR., SCHNEIDER, D. M., TOMKINS, S. S. (1965). *Aspects of Family Structure*. Princeton: Princeton University Press. Two items of interest to fertility: first, Coale's calculation of average household size under different assumptions of marriage pattern and residence of young married couples; and second, the debate between Levy and Fallers, the former arguing that family size is demographically determined, the latter that a process of 'fictionalising' takes place when demographic supply inadequate to needs of kin group. Fallers' essay is an excellent caution against the naive sociological assumption that family structure is demographically-determined in any simple sense, and contains, latently, an interesting hypothesis to explain persisting high fertility in developing societies when mortality is reduced. A most important debate; see also FOX (1967); LEIBENSTEIN (1957).

COALE, A. J., TYE, C. Y. (1961). 'The significance of age-patterns of fertility in high-fertility populations', *Milbank Memorial Fund Quarterly* 39: 631–46. Showing that a rise in the age at marriage in a country such as India could lead to a later age at childbearing, a sizeable reduction in natality and a check on population growth. See AGARWALA (1967); DAS (1967); TALWAR (1967).

COALE, A. J., ZELNIK, M. (1963). *New Estimates of Fertility and Population in the United States.* Princeton: Princeton University Press. A reconstruction of American historical rates, 1855–1960. See MAULDIN (1966); YASUBA (1962).

COLE, L. C. (1965). 'Dynamics of animal population growth', *in* SHEPS, RIDLEY, (1965): 221–41. A comparative analysis of some features of the demography of human and non-human animals; especially interesting for the comparative discussion of the effects on fertility of different ages of maturation ('ages at marriage') and on population growth of different mortality rates. See WYNNE–EDWARDS (1962).

COLEMAN, J. C., KATZ, E., MENZEL, H. (1957). 'The diffusion of an innovation among physicians', *Sociometry* 20: 253–70. A standard case history of a diffusing innovation (a new drug), illustrating the assumptions behind and nature of diffusion models. See CARLSSON (1966–7); ROGERS (1961); BESHERS (1967).

COLLVER, A. O. (1965). *Birth Rates in Latin America: New Estimates of Historical Trends and Fluctuations.* Research Series no. 7, Institute of International Studies, Berkeley: University of California Press. A useful additional source to the U.N. *Demographic Yearbook* for one of the demographically most alarming areas of the world. See MORTARA (1964).

COLLVER, A., SPEARE, A., LIU, P. (1966–7). 'Local variations of fertility in Taiwan', *Population Studies* 20: 329–42. See also TAUBER (1961); FREEDMAN, PEN, TAKESHITA and SUN (1963); FREEDMAN, TAKESHITA and SUN (1964); FREEDMAN (1965); TAKE-SHITA (1966; 1967); and, for a review of the birth control programmes on the island, BERELSON, FREEDMAN (1964); CHOW *et al.* (1968). For the significance of Taiwan, see text.

COMBS, J. W. (1954). 'Human fertility in Puerto Rico', Ph.D. Columbia University, 1954, *Dissertation Abstracts* 14: 2430–1. Discusses fertility trends, including differentials, from 1899 to 1950s.

CONCEPCION, M. B. (1967). 'The effect of current social and economic changes in the developing countries on differential fertility', *in* UNITED NATIONS DEPARTMENT OF ECONOMIC AND SOCIAL AFFAIRS: *World Population Conference* 1965, II, New York: United Nations, 124–7. A brief but useful summary article.

CONNELL, K. H. (1950). *Population of Ireland, 1750–1845.* Oxford: Clarendon Press. See text; and GLASS (1953); DAVIS (1963); DRAKE (1963). CONNELL has summarised his thesis in GLASS, EVERSLEY (1965).

COX, P. R. (1966). *Demography.* Cambridge: Cambridge University Press. The latest edition of the standard English text. See BARCLAY (1958); BOGUE (1969).

DANDEKAR, K. (1959). *A Demographic Survey of Six Rural Communities.* Poona: Gokhale Institute of Politics and Economics. See below.

DANDEKAR, K. (1963). 'Analysis of birth intervals of a set of women', *Eugenics Quarterly* 10: 73–8. Two sources of data for calculations of natural fertility, rates of which are calculated from historical populations, some developing societies, or modern isolates. See BOURGEOIS–PICHAT (1965a; 1965b); GAUTIER, HENRY (1958); HENRY (1965b); EATON, MAYER (1953); SHEPS (1965–6); SMITH (1960); TIETZE (1957).

DAS, N. C. (1967). 'A note on the effect of postponement of marriage on fertility', *in* UNITED NATIONS DEPARTMENT OF ECONOMIC AND SOCIAL AFFAIRS: *World Population Conference* 1965, II, New York: United Nations: 128–31. The Indian case; see text. Also AGARWALA (1967; 1957); TALWAR (1967); COALE, TYE (1961).

DAVIDSON, D. (1963). 'Actions, reasons and causes', *Journal of Philosophy* 60: 685–700. Also *in* WHITE (1968). A concise summary of the argument that reasons can be causes; see text (Chs. IV, VI); MACINTYRE (1967); summary by WHITE in WHITE (1968). Opposing case familiar to sociologists: WINCH (1958).

DAVIS, K. (1955a). 'Institutional patterns favouring high fertility in underdeveloped areas', *Eugenics Quarterly* 2. See also FREEDMAN (1963); LORIMER (1954); LEIBEN-STEIN (1957).

DAVIS, K. (1955b). 'Malthus and the theory of population', *in* LAZARSFELD, P. F., ROSENBERG, M. (eds.): *The Language of Social Research*. Glencoe: Free Press: 540–53. An examination of the logic of Malthus' theory. See FLEW (1957).

DAVIS, K. (1963). 'The theory of change and response in modern demographic history', *Population Index* 29: 345–66. A sophisticated examination of the demographic aspects of the 'demographic transition'. Argues that too simple to assume that fertility eventually falls in response to fall in mortality; a satisfactory *theory* of the demographic transition will depend on an understanding of what particular intervening variables vary to lower fertility. Takes the cases of Ireland and Japan as examples of a 'multi-phasic' response, involving more than one such variable. Does not consider the now considerable evidence to suggest that the transition in fertility rates may have started in some countries *before* mortality fell; nevertheless, his point that the demographic responses will vary with cultural vatiations still stands. For a review of the intervening variables concerned, see text and DAVIS, BLAKE (1956).

DAVIS, K. (1967). 'Population policy: will current programmes succeed?', *Science* 158 (November 10): 730–9. A sceptical comment on current optimisms about family planning in developing countries, with special reference to trends in ideal family size.

DAVIS, K., BLAKE, J. (1955–6). 'Social structure and fertility: an analytic framework', *Economic Development and Cultural Change* 4: 211–35. See text. The article also discussess, briefly, the relationships between the intermediate variables and certain social factors.

DAVTYAN, L. M. (1967). 'The influence of socio-economic factors on natality (as exemplified in the Armenian Soviet Socialist Republic,) *in* UNITED NATIONS DEPARTMENT OF ECONOMIC AND SOCIAL AFFAIRS: *World Population Conference* 1965, II, New York: United Nations: 73–7. See also SADVOKASOVA (1967); URLANIS (1967); HEER (1968); MAZUR (1967).

DAY, L. H. (1968). 'Natality and ethnocentrism: some relationships suggested by an analysis of Catholic–Protestant differentials', *Population Studies* 22: 27–50. See text; thesis was suggested by VAN HEEK (1956).

DE JONG, G. F. (1965). 'Religious fundamentalism, socio-economic status and fertility attitudes in the Southern Appalachians', *Demography* 2: 540–8. Higher fertility preferred in low socio-economic status, older, more fundamentalist; see FORD, DE JONG (1963–4).

DEMENY, P. (1968a). 'Early fertility decline in Austria-Hungary: a lesson in demographic transition', *Proceedings of the American Academy of Arts and Sciences* 97: 502–22. See text. Demeny adopts the methodology suggested by COALE (1967); for similar analyses, see MATRAS (1965a; 1965b; 1965–6); VAN DE WALLE (1968).

DEMENY, P., BRASS, W. (eds.) (1968b). *The Demography of Tropical Africa*. Princeton: Princeton University Press. A collection of strictly demographic papers on the most 'primitive' demographic structures in the world, and ones for which statistical records are poorest.

DEVEREUX, G. (1955). *A Study of Abortion in Primitive Societies*, London: Gollancz. Subtitled 'a typological, distributional and dynamic analysis of the prevention of birth in 400 pre-industrial societies'; makes no attempt to assess the demographic significance of abortion. Suspiciously, only finds one clear negative report on abortion in a primitive society. Despite cloudy and dubious psychoanalytical interpretations of abortion, a useful source of information. See also NAG (1962); CARR-SAUNDERS (1922); FORD (1945).

DICE, L. R. (1965). 'Relation of fertility to religious affiliation and church attendance in Ann Arbor, Michigan, 1951–4', *Eugenics Quarterly* 12: 102–11. See LENSKI (1963).

DONAYRE, J. (1966). 'Population growth and fertility at high altitude', *in* PAN-AMERICAN HEALTH ORGANISATION, Scientific Publication 140, *Life at High Altitudes*. Washington D.C.: P.–A. H. O.: 74–93. See JAMES (1966–7); WHITEHEAD (1968).

DOUGLAS, M. (1966). 'Population control in primitive groups', *British Journal of Sociology* 17: 263–73. See text (Ch. IV); CARR–SAUNDERS (1922).

DRAKE, M. (1963). 'Marriage and population growth in Ireland, 1750–1845', *Economic History Review* 2nd ser. 16: 301–13. Challenges Connell's assumption of early marriage in 18th c. See CONNELL (1950; 1965); GLASS (1953); DAVIS (1963).

DRAKE, M. (1969). *Population and Society in Norway. 1735–1865,* Cambridge: Cambridge University Press. First-class study with much socio-economic detail on differences within rural economy and their demographic implications. Uses qualitative material from Sundt and Malthus and challenges latter, as well as available statistics. Considerable sociological value.

DRIVER, E. D. (1963). *Differential Fertility in Central India,* Princeton: Princeton University Press. A sample of 2,589 heads of households in Nagpur district. The study includes much information on both intervening and independent variables, and is perhaps one of the most thorough on India.

DUESENBERRY, J. S. (1960). 'Comment', *in* UNIVERSITIES–NATIONAL BUREAU COMMITTEE FOR ECONOMIC RESEARCH: *Demographic and Economic Change in Developed Countries.* Princeton: Princeton University Press: 231–4. See text; and BECKER (1960); EASTERLIN (1969); BLAKE (1968).

DUNCAN, O. D. (1964). 'Residential areas and differential fertility', *Eugenics Quarterly* 11: 82–9. See text; a re-analysis of Indianapolis data (see WHELPTON, KISER, 1946, 1950, 1952, 1954, 1958).

DUNCAN, O. D. (1965). 'Farm background and differential fertility', *Demography* 2: 240–9. Sample as BLAU AND DUNCAN (1967). Corroborates GOLDBERG (1958–9) in important finding that farm origin plus low educational achievement leads to high fertility, and that either two generations of urban residence or high levels of education are sufficient for 'controlled fertility'.

DUNCAN, O. D. (1966). 'Methodological issues in the analysis of social mobility', in SMELSER, N. J., LIPSET, S. M. (eds.): *Social Structure and Social Mobility in Economic Development.* Chicago: Aldine, London: Routledge and Kegan Paul. Extremely important: see text, and BERENT (1951–2); BLAU, DUNCAN (1967).

DUNCAN, O. D., FREEDMAN, R., COBLE, J. M., SLESINGER, D. P. (1965). 'Marital fertility and size of family of orientation', *Demography* 2: 508–15. CPS data. Finds a small association; see BERENT (1953).

EASTERLIN, R. A. (1962). *The American Baby Boom in Historical Perspective.* New York: National Bureau of Economic Research, Occasional Paper no. 79. See text; EASTERLIN (1966; 1969). Also *in* HEER (1968c).

EASTERLIN, R. A. (1966). 'On the relation of economic factors to recent and projected fertility changes', *Demography* 3: 131–53. See text; EASTERLIN (1962; 1969).

EASTERLIN, R. A. (1969). 'Towards a socio-enonomic theory of fertility: a survey of recent research on economic factors in American fertility', *in* BEHRMAN. Best exposition to date of contribution that utility analysis can make to fertility, and thus an essential source. See EASTERLIN (1962; 1966); BLAKE (1967a; 1968); CAMPBELL (1967); FERBER (1966); D. FREEDMAN (1963); FREEDMAN, COOMBS (1966a; 1966b); SCHNEIDER, KRUPP (1965).

EATON, J. W., MAYER, A. J. (1953). 'The social biology of very high fertility amongst the Hutterites: the demography of a unique population', *Human Biology* 25–6: 206–64; also published as *Man's Capacity to Reproduce.* Glencoe: Free Press, 1954. See also DANDEKAR (1959; 1963); and SHEPS (1965–6); TIETZE (1957); JAMES (1963–4; 1964–5); BODMER, JACQUARD (1968).

'ÉTUDE de l'effect sur la natalité française de l'adoption d'une politique plus libérale en matière de régulation des naissances' (1966), *Population* 21: 647–76. See also BLAYO (1968); FEBVAY (1960); MICHEL (1967); PAILLAT (1962); PRESSAT (1967; 1969); SUTTER, BASTIDE (1963).

EVERSLEY, D. E. C. (1959). *Social Theories of Fertility and the Malthusian Debate.* Oxford: Clarendon Press. Standard source, together with U.N. (1953), of classical theories. Pays particular attention to Malthus and standard of living theory, but does not refer to modern empirical work.

FAMILY PLANNING ASSOCIATION (1966). *Abortion in Britain.* London: Pitman Medical Publishing Co. A collection of 23 papers on various aspects of abortion in Britain given at a conference in 1966 (before the Abortion Act became law). Contains, however, remarkably little information on its incidence and social distribution. An estimate of 200,000 per year is mentioned.

FARLEY, R. (1965). 'The demographic rates and social institutions of the nineteenth century Negro population: a stable population analysis', *Demography* 2: 386–98. United States. High nineteenth century fertility ascribed to poor social control mechanisms.

FARLEY, R. (1966). 'Recent changes in Negro fertility', *Demography* 3: 188–203. Includes a discussion of the increasing Negro-white differential in the U.S.

FEBVAY, M. (1960). 'Niveau et évolution de la fécondité par catégorie socio-professionnelle en France', INTERNATIONAL UNION FOR THE SCIENTIFIC STUDY OF POPULATION, *International Population Conference* 1959, I, Vienna: Selbtsverlag: 257–72. See also GLASS (1968); WRONG (1958a; 1958b; 1960); and BLAYO (1968); 'Étude . . .' (1966); MICHEL (1967); PAILLAT (1962); PRESSAT (1967); SUTTER, BASTIDE (1963).

FEDERICI, N. (1968). 'The influence of women's employment on fertility', *in* SZABADY, E. (ed.): *World Views of Population Problems*. Budapest: Akadémiai Kaidó: 77–82. An Italian study. See text (Ch. VI) for discussion and other references.

FERBER, R. (1966). 'Research on household behaviour', *in* AMERICAN ECONOMIC ASSOCIATION, ROYAL ECONOMIC SOCIETY: *Surveys of Economic Theory, III: Resource Allocation*. London: Macmillan, New York: St. Martin's Press: 114–54. A standard summary article, itself carrying an extensive bibliography, of the theory and data on the topic. Of interest to the present discussion are the following sections: (i) theories of spending or saving behaviour, including the absolute income hypothesis, the relative income hypothesis, and the permanent income hypothesis; (ii) influences other than income on spending and saving; (iii) determinants of asset holdings; (iv) determinants of specific expenditures; (v) decision processes; See also BECKER (1960); DUESENBERRY (1960); EASTERLIN (1969); MINCER (1963). SIMON (1966). A simpler introduction than FRIEDMAN's seminal work (1957).

FIRTH, R. (1936). *We, the Tikopia: a Sociological Study of Kinship in Primitive Polynesia*. London: Allen and Unwin.

FIRTH, R. (1959). *Social Change in Tikopia.* London: Allen and Unwin.

FIRTH, R., BORRIE, W. D., SPILLIUS, J. (1956–57). 'Population of Tikopia: 1929–52', *Population Studies* 10: 229–52. Probably the best-documented primitive society from the demographic point of view.

FLEW, A. (1957). 'The structure of Malthus' population theory', *Australasian Journal of Philosophy* 35: 1–20. An examination of the logic of Malthus' theory. See DAVIS (1955).

FORD, C. S. (1945). *A Comparative Study of Human Reproduction*, New Haven: Yale University Press.

FORD, C. S. (1952). 'Control of conception in cross-cultural perspective', *Annals of the New York Academy of Sciences* 54: 763–8. Scattered evidence on contraception, pregnancy and child-bearing brought together from the Yale Human Relations Area Files. See NAG (1962).

FORD, T. R., DE JONG, G. F. (1963). 'The decline of fertility in the southern Appalachian mountain region', *Social Forces* 42: 89–96. Data for 1930, '40, '50 and '60. Finds fertility decline associated with high net out-migration of young adults and intrinsic decrease in metropolitan and prosperous rural areas. See DE JONG (1965).

FOX, R. (1967). *Kinship and marriage*. London: Penguin. A standard anthropological account that makes slight reference to demographically relevant factors (see, e.g., p. 230); see also text, and COALE *et al.* (1965); LORIMER (1954); NAG (1967); BLAKE (1967b).

FREEDMAN, D. (1963). 'The relation of economic status to fertility', *American Economic Review* 53: 414–27. An important study, using the concept of relative income, based on D.A.S. data: see text; KUNZ (1965).

FREEDMAN, M. (1962). 'The Jewish population of Great Britain', *Jewish Journal of Sociology* 4: 95. Includes data on fertility: see GOLDSCHNEIDER (1965; 1965–6; 1967).

FREEDMAN, R. (1961–2). 'The sociology of human fertility', *Current Sociology* 10/11, 2:

35–121. A review of speculation and research to the end of 1961, with an annotated bibliography of 636 items. An essential work of reference.

FREEDMAN, R. (1963). 'Norms for family size in underdeveloped areas', *Proceedings of the Royal Society*, B 159 Part 974: 220–45. A general review, placing especial emphasis on the importance of literacy; see DAVIS (1955); LORIMER (1954); HEER (1966). Also *in* HEER (1968c).

FREEDMAN, R. (1965). 'The accelerating fertility decline in Taiwan', *Population Index* 31: 430–35. See also TAUBER (1961); TAKESHITA (1966; 1967); COLLVER, SPEARE, LIU (1966–7); BERELSON, FREEDMAN (1964). And text.

FREEDMAN, R. (1966). 'Family planning programmes today: major themes of the conference', *in* BERELSON (1966): 811–25. A useful general overview, concentrating on the problems rather than the details of results so far.

FREEDMAN, R., BAUMERT, G., BOLTE, M. (1958–9). 'Expected family size and family size values in West Germany', *Population Studies* 13: 136–50. A particularly good source on ideal, desired and expected family sizes in a European society. See GLASS (1962); SCHWARTZ (1965).

FREEDMAN, R., COALE, A. J. (1966). 'Fertility expectations in the United States: 1962–64', *Population Index* 32: 181–97.

FREEDMAN, R., COOMBS, L. (1966a). 'Childspacing and family economic position', *American Sociological Review* 31: 631–48. See note for FREEDMAN, COOMBS (1966b).

FREEDMAN, R., COOMBS, L. (1966b). 'Economic considerations in family growth decisions', *Population Studies* 20: 197–222. Important studies, based on Detroit Area Study data, finding a complex series of relationships between expected permanent income and family size and spacing, the latter being most strongly affected. See text; and D. FREEDMAN (1963).

FREEDMAN, R., COOMBS, L., FRIEDMAN, J. (1966). 'Social correlates of foetal mortality', *Milbank Memorial Fund Quarterly* 44: 327–44. See also JAMES (1969); STOTT (1962).

FREEDMAN, R., GOLDBERG, D., SHARP, H. (1955). ' "Ideals" about family size in the Detroit Metropolitan Area: 1954', *Milbank Memorial Fund Quarterly* 23: 187–97. An early study. See text.

FREEDMAN, R., PENG, J. Y., TAKESHITA, J. Y., SUN, T. H. (1962–3). 'Fertility trends in Taiwan: tradition and change', *Population Studies* 16: 219–36.

FREEDMAN, R., SLESINGER, D. (1961–2). 'Fertility differentials for the indigenous non-farm population of the U.S.', *Population Studies* 15: 161–73. 1955 GAF data (FREEDMAN, WHELPTON AND CAMPBELL, 1959). Finds that traditional negative relationship between fertility and economic status in U.S. may largely be attributed to relationship among farm-reared population. See also DUNCAN (1965); GOLDBERG (1958–9).

FREEDMAN, R., TAKESHITA, J. Y., SUN, T. H. (1964–5). 'Fertility and family planning in Taiwan: a case study of the demographic transition', *American Journal of Sociology* 70: 16–27.

FREEDMAN, R., WHELPTON, P. K., CAMPBELL, A. A. (1959). *Family Planning, Sterility, and Population Growth*. New York: McGraw–Hill. The first report of the Growth of American Families Project. The fertility performance and expectations of a sample of 2,713 married white women between 18 and 39, tabulated by demographic and socio-economic variables. Together with the second report, WHELPTON et al. (1966), an essential source on the sociology of fertility in the United States.

FREEDMAN, R., WHELPTON, P. K., SMIT, J. W. (1961). 'Socio-economic factors in religious differentials in fertility', *American Sociological Review* 26: 608. See text (Ch. V).

FRENCH, F. E., BIERMAN, J. M. (1962). 'Probabilities of foetal mortality', *Public Health Reports* 77: 835–84. Data from continuous observation of some 3000 Hawaiian pregnancies between 1953 and 1956. Together with SHAPIRO et al. (1962), the only source on foetal mortality in the first six months of pregnancy, and thus crucial evidence for calculations of effective fecundability and natural fertility.

FRIEDLANDER, S., SILVER, M. (1967). 'A quantitative study of the determinants of fertility behaviour', *Demography* 4: 30–70. Regressions run on data from 18 developed, 20 'intermediate' and 47 underdeveloped countries on 25 independent variables against birth rates. See text; and ADELMAN (1963); ADELMAN, MORRIS (1965–66); HEER (1966); RUSSETT *et al.*, (1964); WEINTRAUB (1962).

FRIEDMAN, M. (1967). *A Theory of the Consumption Function*. National Bureau of Economic Research, General Series no. 63, Princeton: Princeton University Press. The standard work on the topic, and especially interesting for the discussion of the concept of permanent (or potential) income. See BECKER (1960); DUESENBERRY (1960); EASTERLIN (1969); FERBER (1966).

GALBRAITH, V. L., THOMAS, P. S. (1941). 'Birth rates and the interwar business cycles', *Journal of the American Statistical Association* 36: 465–76. A classic study, finding an especially good association between cycles and marriage rates. See text, and KIRK, NORTMAN (1958); KIRK (1960); SILVER (1965; 1965–66); TELLA (1960). RYDER (1969) has now placed the interwar period in the U.S. in demographic perspective.

GAUTIER, E., HENRY, L. (1958). *La Population de Crulai, Paroisse Normande*. Paris: Presses Universitaires de France. A demographic reconstruction of a Normandy village between 1674 and 1742. The first of the now numerous monographs on pre-industrial French populations. See also HENRY (1965a; 1965b); and for a review of the French historical work, HENRY (1968). Also WRIGLEY (1969).

GEBHARD, P. H., POMEROY, W. B., MARTIN, C. E., CHRISTENSON, C. V. (1959). *Pregnancy Birth and Abortion*. London: Heinemann. A very thorough study of the sexual histories, including abortions (if any), of 5,293 white non-prison American females and 572 Negro non-prison females, together with 309 Negro women and 900 white women interviewed in prison. The interview is similar to Kinsey (1948; 1953). The sample is not such as to indicate the incidence of abortion in the U.S.A., but nevertheless contains material of sociological interest, including tabulations by parity, age and education.

GENDELL, M. (1967). 'Fertility and development in Brazil', *Demography* 4: 143–57. See text; a study of the country often assumed not to have followed the transition model.

GENERAL REGISTER OFFICE (1917; 1923). *Census of England and Wales 1911, Vol. XIII, Fertility of Marriage*, London: His Majesty's Stationery Office, Part I; Part II. The first detailed record of fertility. See BANKS (1954); GLASS (1938); MATRAS (1965–66).

GENERAL REGISTER OFFICE (1966). *Census 1961, England and Wales: Fertility Tables*. London: H. M. S. O. Most detailed source of fertility statistics for England and Wales; for other areas, see GENERAL REGISTER OFFICE (annual). Tabulates women married once only by fertility, age, duration of marriage, husband's age, husband's socio-economic group, husband's industry group and terminal education age of both partners. Also provides information on remarried women and infertility. See GENERAL REGISTER OFFICE (in preparation).

GENERAL REGISTER OFFICE: *The Registrar General's Statistical Review of England and Wales*, volumes II and III, London: H. M. S. O., annual. Volume II contains the current fertility statistics for the year in question, and they are commented upon in volume III (Commentary). Volume III is usually published three years after the year to which the data refer. 1965, III, was published in 1968; the relevant pages are 46–73. See GENERAL REGISTER OFFICE (1966). Publications similar to those prepared by the Registrar General for England and Wales are also issued by the General Register Office, Edinburgh, and the General Register Division of the Ministry of Finance of the Government of Northern Ireland.

GENERAL REGISTER OFFICE: *Family Intentions Survey* (in preparation). A survey, the fieldwork for which was carried out for the G. R. O. in 1967 by the Government Social Survey and which is presently (1969) being analysed, to determine the fertility expectations of a sample of 6,500 married women under 44 who have been married once only. The analysis will concentrate on a principle component analysis of attitudes to and intentions about fertility; a tabular analysis of contraceptive practice; and a tabular analysis of expectations by cohort (marriage) and generation (birth). See WHELPTON, CAMPBELL, PATTERSON (1966); RYDER, WESTOFF (1967).

GLASS, D. V. (1938). 'Changes in fertility in England and Wales, 1851 to 1931', *in* HOGBEN, L. (ed.): *Political Arithmetic*. London: Allen & Unwin: 161–212. A good source for the period.

GLASS, D. V. (1940). *Population Policies and Movements in Europe*. Oxford: Clarendon Press; reprinted with a new introduction, London: Cass, 1967. A standard source for the period to the Second World War.

GLASS, D. V. (1953). 'Malthus and the limitation of population growth', *in* GLASS, D. V. (ed.): *Introduction to Malthus*. London: Watts. Contains a good discussion of the demography of Ireland before and after the famine; see CONNELL (1950); DAVIS (1963); DRAKE (1963).

GLASS, D. V. (1962). 'Family limitation in Europe: a survey of recent studies', *in* KISER, C, V, (ed.): *Research in Family Planning*. Princeton: Princeton University Press: 231–61. A review of data on European ideal family sizes. See GLASS (1968).

GLASS, D. V. (1968). 'Fertility trends in Europe since the Second World War', *Population Studies* 22: 103–46, and *in* BEHRMAN (1969). A summary of census and survey data. See GLASS (1962).

GLASS, D. V., EVERSLEY, D. E. C. (eds.) (1965). *Population in History*. London: Arnold. A collection of standard papers, giving a good conspectus. For a more integrated presentation see WRIGLEY (1969).

GLASS, D. V., GREBENIK, E. (1954). 'The trend and pattern of fertility in Great Britain', *Papers of the Royal Commission on Population, VI*, Part I: Report, Part II: Tables, London: H. M. S. O. The first, and still the most thorough, cohort analysis of British fertility. An essential source. See also WHELPTON (1954).

GOLDBERG, D. (1958). 'Family role structure and fertility', Ph.D. University of Michigan, 1958, *Dissertation Abstracts* 19: 595–6. See also RAINWATER (1965).

GOLDBERG, D. (1958–9). 'The fertility of two-generation urbanites', *Population Studies* 12: 214–22. An extremely important article, from D.A.S. data. See text, and DUNCAN (1965); FREEDMAN, SLESINGER (1961–2).

GOLDBERG, D. (1960). 'Another look at the Indianapolis fertility data', *Milbank Memorial Fund Quarterly* 38: 23–36. See text; DUNCAN (1965); GOLDBERG(1958–9); and WHELPTON, KISER (1946; 1950; 1952; 1954; 1958).

GOLDBERG, D. (1967). 'Some observations on recent changes in American fertility based on sample survey data', *Eugenics Quarterly* 14. Concludes that changes in spacing have probably been the key factor in the decline of period fertility; see also RYDER (1969).

GOLDBERG, D., COOMBS, C. H. (1963). 'Some applications of unfolding theory to fertility analysis', *in* MILBANK MEMORIAL FUND: *Emerging Techniques in Population Research*. New York: Milbank Memorial Fund. See text (Ch. IV). Coombs' ideas about measurement, and particularly his attempts to produce scales that are basically only ordinal but have some of the properties of interval scales, are elaborated in his *A Theory of Data*, New York: Wiley, 1964.

GOLDSCHNEIDER, C. (1965). 'Nativity, generation and Jewish fertility', *Sociological Analysis* 26: 137–47. See text (Ch. V); and GOLDSCHNEIDER (1965–6; 1967); FREEDMAN, WHELPTON, SMIT (1961).

GOLDSCHNEIDER, C. (1965–6). 'Trends in Jewish fertility', *Sociology and Social Research* 50: 173–86. See text; and GOLDSCHNEIDER (1965; 1967); FREEDMAN, WHELPTON, SMIT (1961).

GOLDSCHNEIDER, C. (1967). 'Fertility of the Jews', *Demography* 4: 196–209. See text; and GOLDSCHNEIDER (1965; 1965–6); FREEDMAN, WHELPTON, SMIT (1961).

GOLDSTEIN, S., MAYER, K. (1964). 'Population decline and the social and demographic structure of an American city', *American Sociological Review* 29: 48–54. The city is Providence, R.I.

GOLDSTEIN, S., MAYER, K. (1965). 'Residence and status differences in fertility', *Milbank Memorial Fund Quarterly* 43: 291–310. 1960 Census tracts, R.I. Positive relationship between closer spacing, high status, and suburban residence. For more exact analysis of the urban fertility pattern in the U.S., see DUNCAN (1965); GOLDBERG (1958–9; 1960); FREEDMAN, SLESINGER (1961–2).

GOOD, D. (1964). 'Some aspects of fertility change in Hungary', *Population Index* 30: 131–74. For the importance of Hungary, see text. See also MEHLAN (1966); A. N., R. Pr. (1965); SRB (1964); SZABADY *et al.* (1966); and SZABADY (1964).

GREBENIK, E., ROWNTREE, G. (1963). 'Factors associated with the age at marriage in Britain', *Proceedings of the Royal Society*, Series B, 159, Part 974: 178–98 (discussion: 198–202). An analysis of data from the sample surveyed for Rowntree and Pierce (1961–2); contains information on age at marriage by social class for selected cohorts interviewed in 1959–60. Finds no strongly associated factors that may be explanatory, but confesses that this may be a function of the research design rather than of the substantive situation. See RELE (1965).

GRUNER, R. (1966). 'Teleological and functional explanations', *Mind* 75: 516–26. An excellent account of the logic of the two, arguing that they are both (different) partial forms of normal deductive explanation. See HARRÉ (1961); WHITE (1968).

GUPTA, P. B., MALAKER, C. R. (1963). 'Fertility differentials with levels of living and adjustment of fertility, birth and death rates', *Sankhyā* (Calcutta) B 25: 23–48. Data from seventh round, rural, of the National Sample Survey (c. 1,000 villages; 500 sample blocks in towns and cities). 'The working hypothesis . . . is that with an increasing standard of living, the fertility rate should rise to a maximum, fall to a minimum, and again rise to attain an optimum value'; confirmed with data available. An extremely important illustration of the argument adopted by LORIMER (1967); see also LEIBENSTEIN (1957).

HABBAKUK, H. J. (1955). 'Family structure and economic change in nineteenth-century Europe', *Journal of Economic History* 15: 1–12. Discusses the association between inheritance patterns and fertility.

HAJNAL, J. (1953). 'Age at marriage and proportions marrying', *Population Studies* 7: 111–36. A standard article on the 'marriage boom' of post-war birth cohorts, in which the mean age at marriage fell. See RYDER (1969).

HAJNAL, J. (1965). 'European marriage patterns in perspective', *in* GLASS, EVERSLEY (1965): 101–43. A first-class summary of the evidence and evaluation of its significance on the proposition that the age at marriage in Europe between about 1600 and the twentieth century was higher than that recorded for any other population. See text (Ch. III). For an argument, which HAJNAL rejects, that the medieval population also married somewhat late, see RUSSELL (1948).

HALL, M.-F. (1965). 'Birth control in Lima, Peru: attitudes and practices', *Milbank Memorial Fund Quarterly* 43: 409–38. A good study. See also the relevant sections in BERELSON (1966).

HARRÉ, R. (1961). *Theories and Things, a brief study in prescriptive metaphysics*. London: Sheed and Ward. A concise, complex, persuasive criticism of extreme positivism.

HART, H. L. A., HONORÉ, A. (1959). *Causation in the Law*, Oxford: Clarendon Press. See text, Ch. IV; also DAVIDSON (1963); MACINTYRE (1967); WHITE (1968).

HAUSER, P. M. (1962). 'On design for experiment and research in fertility control', *in* KISER, P. V. (ed.): *Research in Family Planning*. Princeton: Princeton University Press: 463–74. An interesting model of factors affecting fertility control which nevertheless works within the conventions of traditional survey analysis. See also HILL (1968).

HAUSER, P. M., DUNCAN, O. D. (eds.) (1959). *The Study of Population: an Inventory and Appraisal*. Chicago and London: University of Chicago Press. A standard introduction of 33 articles, particularly concerned with the international organisation of academic population studies. RYDER's chapter 'Fertility' is especially good; see also RYDER (1965). MOORE's chapter 'Sociology and Demography', however, is a mechanical and unthinking essay in simple functionalism of the most misleading kind.

HAWLEY, A. H. (1955). 'Rural fertility in central Luzon', *American Sociological Review* 20: 21–27. Positive relation between fertility and size of holding; see STYS (1957–58).

HAWLEY, A. H., PRACHUABMOH, V. (1966). 'Family growth and family planning in a rural district of Thailand', *in* BERELSON (1966): 523–44. A good study of the social correlates of the adoption of family planning.

10

HAWTHORN, G. P., BUSFIELD, N. J. (1968). 'Some social determinants of family size: report of a pilot study', University of Essex, mimeo. First report of a study of couples in a representative English town to test some of the ideas developed in this book.

HEATH, A. (1968). 'Economic theory and sociology', *Sociology* 2: 273–92. A critique of BLAU (1964).

HEER, D. M. (1964–65). 'Fertility differences between Indian and Spanish-speaking parts of Andean countries', *Population Studies* 18: 71–84. See HEER, TURNER (1964–65); and STYCOS (1962–63); JAMES (1966–67); HEER (1967); WHITEHEAD (1968); BRADSHAW (1969); also discussion in text (Ch. V.)

HEER, D. M. (1966). 'Economic development and fertility', *Demography* 3: 423–44. A most important article: see text. Also ADELMAN (1963); ADELMAN, MORRIS (1965–66); FRIEDLANDER, SILVER (1967); RUSSETT *et al.* (1964).

HEER, D. M. (1967). 'Fertility differences in Andean countries: a reply to W. H. James', *Population Studies* 21: 71–73. See HEER (1964–65); HEER, TURNER (1964–65); STYCOS (1962–63); JAMES (1966–67); WHITEHEAD (1968); BRADSHAW (1969); also discussion in text (Ch. V.)

HEER, D. M. (1968a). 'The demographic transition in the Russian Empire and the Soviet Union', *Journal of Social History* 1: 193–240. A good synoptic description and tentative explanation of one demographic transition of unusual interest; see DAVIS (1963); and PETERSEN (1961); LORIMER (1946); BRACKETT (1962).

HEER, D. M. (1968b). *Society and Population*. Englewood Cliffs, N. J., London: Prentice-Hall. A good general introductory discussion.

HEER, M. (ed.) (1968c). *Readings on Population*. Englewood Cliffs, N. J., London: Prentice-Hall. A companion to the previous item.

HEER, D. M., TURNER, E. S. (1964–65). 'Area differences in Latin American fertility', *Population Studies* 18: 279–92. See HEER (1964–65); STYCOS (1962–63); JAMES (1966–67); HEER (1967); WHITEHEAD (1968); BRADSHAW (1969); see text (Ch. V).

HENIN, R. A. (1968). 'Fertility differentials in the Sudan', *Population Studies* 22: 147–64.

HENRIPIN, J. (1954). *La Population Canadienne au debut du XVIIIe Siècle*. Paris: Presses Universitaires de France. The demography of a population with very high fertility; for a comparable situation in metropolitan France, see: P. GOUBERT: 'Legitimate fecundity and infant mortality in France during the eighteenth century: a comparison', *Proceedings of the American Academy of Arts and Sciences* 97 (1968): 593–603. See also HENRY (1965); CARISSE (1964).

HENRY, L. (1956). *Anciennes Familles Genevoises*. Paris:. Presses Universitaires de France. A classic historical study.

HENRY, L. (1961). 'Some data on natural fertility', *Eugenics Quarterly* 8: 81–91.

HENRY, L. (1962). 'A propos d'une enquête sur la contraception en Grande-Bretagne', *Population* 17: 65–74. A critical appraisal of Rowntree and Pierce (1961–62). In particular, cautions against field data on incidence of *coitus interruptus*.

HENRY, L. (1963). 'Aspects biologiques de la fécondité', *Proceedings of the Royal Society*, B, 159: 81–89.

HENRY, L. (1964). 'Mesure de temps mort en fécondité naturelle', *Population* 19: 485–514.

HENRY, L. (1964–65). 'Some comments on W. H. James' article', *Population Studies* 18: 175–80. See JAMES (1963–64; 1964–65).

HENRY, L. (1965a). 'French statistical research in natural fertility', in SHEPS, RIDLEY (1965): 333–50.

HENRY, L. (1965b). 'The population of France in the eighteenth century', *in* GLASS, EVERSLEY (1965): 434–56. See also the articles by GOUBERT, BOURGEOIS-PICHAT and MEUVRET in the same volume; and HENRY (1968).

HENRY, L. (1968). 'Historical demography', *Proceedings of the American Academy of Arts and Sciences* 97: 385–96.

HENRY, L., LEVY, P. (1960). 'Ducs et pairs sous l'Ancien Régime', *Population* 15: 807–30. See, for an approximately equivalent English group, Hollingsworth (1957–58). See also STONE (1961).

HILL, R. (1968). 'Research in human fertility', *International Social Science Journal* 20: 226–62. A useful summary of some recent work, including a brief account of the way in which contributors from different disciplines have affected the fortunes of the understanding of fertility behaviour and fertility control.

HILL, R., STYCOS, J. M., BACK, K. (1959). *The Family and Population Control*. Chapel Hill: University of North Carolina Press. A study of 1,046 lower class wives in Puerto Rico, 1953–55. Sociologically one of the most sophisticated and thorough fertility studies, and especially interesting in that the research team carried out a controlled experiment in contraceptive education to test their analytic model. Intra-familial variables are dealt with in particular detail.

HIMES, N. E. (1936). *A Medical History of Contraception*. Baltimore: Williams and Wilkins; reprinted New York: Gamut Press, 1963. A standard history, although sociologically and demographically deficient, assuming that no contraceptive knowledge was available before industrialisation.

HOFFMAN, L. W., WYATT, F. (1960). 'Social change and motivations for having large families', *Merrill-Palmer Quarterly* 6: 235–44. Argue that changes in women's roles, in parental roles and an increase in amount of loneliness and alienation in American society have all led to larger families; for an elaboration and circumstantial test, see RAINWATER (1965).

HOLLINGSWORTH, T. H. (1957–58). 'A demographic study of the British ducal families', *Population Studies* 11: 4–26; also *in* GLASS, EVERSLEY (1965): 354–78. The cohorts born 1330–1954. See HENRY, LEVY (1960); and HOLLINGSWORTH (1964).

HOLLINGSWORTH, T. H. (1964–65). 'The demography of the British peerage', Supplement to *Population Studies* 18: 108 pp. The cohorts born 1550–1949. See HENRY (1956); HENRY, LEVY (1960); HOLLINGSWORTH (1957).

HOMANS, G. P. (1942). *English Villagers of the Thirteenth Century*. Cambridge: Harvard University Press. Perhaps the most thorough study of marriage in medieval rural society. However, under-estimates high mortality of the period, and thus very probably over-estimates ages at marriage. See HAJNAL (1965); RUSSELL (1948).

HUBBACK, J. (1955). 'The fertility of graduate women', *Eugenics Review* 47: 107–13. Finds higher than average fertility; see KISER FRANK (1967); WESTOFF, POTVIN (1966), for American data.

HUGHES, R. B. (1959). 'Human fertility differentials: the influence of industrial urban development on birth rates', *Population Review* 3: 58–69. Sample of Tennessee farm families; finds positive relation between income and fertility when education and parental status are controlled.

HUTCHINSON, B. (1960–61). 'Fertility, social mobility and urban migration in Brazil', *Population Studies* 14: 182–89. Negative relation between fertility and status and fertility and mobility; not affected by rural/urban origins. See GENDELL (1967); HUTCHINSON (1965).

HUTCHINSON, B. (1965). 'Colour, social status and fertility in Brazil', *América Latina* 8: 3–25. See text; and GENDELL (1967); HUTCHINSON (1960–61).

HYRENIUS, H. (1946). 'The relation between birth rates and economic activity in Sweden, 1920–44', *Bulletin of the Oxford Institute of Statistics* 8: 14–21. A classic study using the unique Swedish census data on income. See also MYRDAL (1941).

JAIN, S. P. (1964). 'Indian fertility: our knowledge and gaps', *Journal of Family Welfare* (Bombay) 11: 6–19. See also AGARWALA (1964); GUPTA, MALAKER (1963); MAYER (1960); NAG (1967); SINHA (1962); SAMUEL (1963); LORIMER (1967); DRIVER (1963).

JAMES, W. H. (1963–64). 'Estimates of fecundability', *Population Studies* 17: 57–65.

JAMES, W. H. (1964–65). 'Fecundability estimates: some comments on M. Henry's paper', *Population Studies* 18: 181–86. See HENRY (1964–65). An intricate and fascinating argument in which JAMES, by using a different method, arrives at fecundability estimates below those produced by other workers, and is challenged by HENRY. The discussion reveals clearly the variables that have to be included in any estimate of fecundability and the weight that they might be given. JAMES' data comes from Hutterite studies; see EATON, MAYER (1953);

TIETZE (1957). SHEPS' (1965–66) paper on the Hutterites had not then been published. See text above; and WOLFERS (1968).

JAMES, W. H. (1966–67). 'The effect of altitude on fertility in Andean countries', *Population Studies* 20: 97–101. See also DONAYRE (1966); and STYCOS (1962–63); HEER (1964–65); HEER, TURNER (1964–65); HEER (1967); WHITEHEAD (1968); BRADSHAW (1969); and discussion in the text (Ch. V).

JAMES, W. H. (1969). 'The effect of maternal psychological stress on the foetus', *British Journal of Psychiatry* 115: 811–25. See STOTT (1962); FREEDMAN, COOMBS, FRIEDMAN (1966).

JOHNSON, G. Z. (1960). 'Differential fertility in European countries', *in* NATIONAL BUREAU OF ECONOMIC RESEARCH: *Demographic and Economic Change in Developed Countries*. Princeton: Princeton University Press: 36–72 (comment by R. FREEDMAN, pp. 72–76). See GLASS (1968); KISER (1960); WRONG (1958b; 1960).

KEYFITZ, N., FLIEGER, W. (1968). *World Population: an analysis of vital data*. Chicago University of Chicago Press. A compendium of data on population, including virtually all the information on birth and death rates available from registration systems around the world, and containing some 800 life tables and other special computations. See also UNITED NATIONS (1965b).

KINSEY, A. (1948). *Sexual Behaviour in the Human Male*. Philadelphia: Saunders.

KINSEY, A. (1953). *Sexual Behaviour in the Human Female*. Philadelphia: Saunders. A standard source on coital frequencies within marriage, which is nevertheless open to some criticism. The frequencies it reports are almost certainly too high for non-Western societies; see BOURGEOIS–PICHAT (1965a). Also HENRY (1963); LACHENBRUCH (1967).

KIRK, D., NORTMAN, D. L. (1958). 'Business and babies: the influence of the business cycle on birth rates', *Proceedings of the Social Sciences Section: American Statistical Association:* 151–60. See text; and KIRK (1960); SILVER (1965; 1965–66); TELLA (1960); GALBRAITH AND THOMAS (1941).

KIRK, D. (1960). 'The influence of business cycles on marriage and birth rates', *in* NATIONAL BUREAU OF ECONOMIC RESEARCH: *Demographic and Economic Change in Developed Countries*. Princeton: Princeton University Press; 241–57 (comment by D. S. THOMAS, pp. 257–60). See text; and GALBRAITH AND THOMAS (1941); KIRK, NORTMAN (1958); SILVER (1965; 1965–66); TELLA (1960).

KIRK, D. (1967). 'Factors affecting Moslem natality', *in* UNITED NATIONS DEPARTMENT OF ECONOMIC AND SOCIAL AFFAIRS: *World Population Conference* 1965, II, New York: United Nations: 149–54. Includes not only a discussion of independent variables (see also RIZK (1963); YAUKEY (1961)) but also of the importance of the intervening variable of polygynous unions; see also SEKLANI (1960). Reprinted, with minor alterations, *in* BERELSON (1966): 561–79.

KISER, C. V. (1960). 'Differential fertility in the United States', *in* NATIONAL BUREAU FOR ECONOMIC RESEARCH: *Demographic and Economic Change in Developed Countries*. Princeton: Princeton University Press: 77–113 (comment by R. GUTMAN, pp. 113–16). A summary article, incorporating only the first G.A.F. data (FREEDMAN, WHELPTON, CAMPBELL, 1959) of that now available from the several American field studies. See also RYDER (1969); GOLDBERG (1967); JOHNSON (1960); WRONG (1958b; 1960).

KISER, C. V. (ed.) (1962). *Research in Family Planning*, Princeton: Princeton University Press. An important collection of papers from a Milbank Memorial Fund conference in 1960. See also BERELSON (1966); BOGUE (1967); BEHRMAN (1969); MURAMATSU, HARPER (1966); SHEPS, RIDLEY (1965).

KISER, C. V. (1968). 'The present status of research on fertility in the United States', *in* SZABADY, E. (ed.): *World Views of Population Problems*. Budapest: Akadémiai Kaidó: 177–83. A summary of research achievements and possibilities; see also TABAH, VIET (1966).

KISER, C. V., FRANK, M. E. (1967). 'Factors associated with the low fertility of non-white women of college attainment', *Milbank Memorial Fund Quarterly* 45: 427–80. 1960 American census data. Of three factors, age at marriage, marital stability and employment status, examined, last found to be most important. See also HUBBACK (1955); WESTOFF, POTVIN (1966).

KISER, C. V., GRABILL, W. H., CAMPBELL, A. A. (1968). *Trends and Variations in Fertility in the United States*. Cambridge: Harvard University Press. An extremely important monograph based on 1960 census data; published too late for its findings to be incorporated into the text above.

KLINGER, A. (1966). 'Abortion programmes', *in* BERELSON (1966): 465–76. Abortion in Eastern Europe (including the U.S.S.R.). See also TIETZE (1965a; 1965b); MEHLAN (1966); GABHARD *et al.* (1959); CALDERONE (1958); FREEDMAN (1966); FAMILY PLANNING ASSOCIATION (1966); SZABADY *et al.* (1966), and references therein.

KRAUSE, J. T. (1967). 'Some aspects of population change, 1690–1790', *in* JONES, E. L., MINGAY, G. (eds.): *Land, Labour and Population*. London: Arnold: 187–205. A recent statement of the nature of the demographic transition in Britain. For recent disputes, see RAZZELL (1965; 1967). See also WRIGLEY (1969).

KROTKI, K., LAPIERRE, E. (1968). 'La fécondité au Canada selon la religion, l'origine ethnique et l'état matrimonial', *Population* 23: 815–34. An extension and confirmation of BURCH (1966) for Canadian fertility in 1961, 1966. See also CARISSE (1964).

KUHN, T. S. (1962). *The Structure of Scientific Revolutions*. Chicago: University of Chicago Press. Thesis that scientific development occurs in uneven bounds from paradigm to paradigm rather than progressively through refutation of successive hypotheses.

KUNZ, P. R. (1965). 'The relation of income and fertility', *Journal of Marriage and the Family* 27: 509–13. Data from 1960 U.S. census, 5% sample: married white women, 35–44, in urban areas. Holding husband's occupation, education constant, positive association between fertility and income. See D. FREEDMAN (1963); FREEDMAN, COOMBS (1966a; 1966b); and income discussion in text Ch. V.

'LA LIMITATION des naissances en France' (1956), *Population* 11: 209–345. See also BERGUES *et al.* (1960); SIEBERT, SUTTER (1964); WEILL-HALLÉ (1967).

LACHENBRUCH, P. A. (1967). 'Frequency and timing of intercourse: the probability of conception', *Population Studies* 21: 5–22.

LAFITTE, F. (1962–63). 'The users of birth control clinics', *Population Studies* 16: 12–30. A British study.

LAURENCE, K. A. (1966). 'Current laboratory studies on fertility regulation: evaluation of their possibilities', *in* BERELSON (1966): 387–95. Briefly describes current experiments that may lead to new human contraceptives.

LEACH, E. R. (1966). 'Virgin birth', *Proceedings of the Royal Anthropological Institute* 1966: 39–50. See SPIRO (1968); correspondence in *Man*, n.s., 3 (1968); 4 (1969) *passim*.

LEGEARD, C. (1966). *Guide de Recherches Documentaires en Démographie*. Paris: Gauthier-Villars. The most useful handbook guide to demography as a field, offering information on primary sources, techniques, bibliography and research centres.

LEIBENSTEIN, H. (1957). *Economic Backwardness and Economic Growth*. New York: Wiley, London: Chapman and Hall: 147–75. A most important thesis; see text; LORIMER (1967).

LENSKI, G. (1963). *The Religious Factor*, Garden City N.Y.: Doubleday. Contains information on fertility from D.A.S. data.

LEVI-STRAUSS, C. (1955). *Tristes Tropiques*. Paris: Plon; translated as *World on the Wane*, London: Hutchinson, 1961. Brilliant, idiosyncratic intellectual autobiography that includes much information on South American Indians, including Nambikwara. The translation, which is bad, omits three chapters.

LEWIS-FANNING, E. (1949). *Report on an Enquiry into Family Limitation and its Influence on Human Fertility during the Past Fifty Years*. Papers of the Royal Commission on Population, I, London: H. M. S. O. Pioneer study on a sample of 10,297 once-married, still-married women in England and Scotland. See text. Similar work is now being carried on by Population Investigation Committee, London School of Economics; see ROWNTREE, PIERCE (1961–62) and current work described in text (Ch. III).

LOCKRIDGE, K. (1968). 'Land, population and the evolution of New England society, 1630–1790', *Past and Present* 39: 62–80. Effects of population pressure on social structure. See STEVENSON (1968).

LORIMER, F. (1946). *The Population of the Soviet Union: History and Prospects.* Geneva: League of Nations. See BRACKETT (1962); HEER (1968a); PETERSEN (1961). Outdated but still of interest. Modern studies include data from 1959 census, the second reliable Soviet assessment (the first was 1926).

LORIMER, F. (1954). *Culture and Human Fertility.* Paris: UNESCO. Still a useful source on fertility and its social and cultural correlates in primitive and agrarian societies. See NAG (1962).

LORIMER, F. (1967). 'The economics of family formation under different conditions', *in* UNITED NATIONS DEPARTMENT OF ECONOMIC AND SOCIAL AFFAIRS: *World Population Conference* 1965, II, New York: United Nations: 92–95. An examination of the household micro-economics that may in part explain transitions in fertility; see text (Ch. V) and LEIBENSTEIN (1957).

LOTKA, A. J. (1925). *The Elements of Physical Biology.* Baltimore: Williams and Wilkins. Classic definition of the concept of 'stability', containing proof that a population subject to constant age-specific mortality and fertility will eventually adopt a stable structure. Technical; best prefaced by more introductory analysis, such as COX (1966).

LUKES, S. (1968). 'Methodological individualism reconsidered', *British Journal of Sociology* 19: 119–29. A criticism of methodological individualism that nevertheless fails to answer certain questions: see text (Ch. VI).

MACINTYRE, A. (1967). 'The idea of a social science', *Aristotelian Society Supplementary Volume* 61: 95–114. A reply to WINCH (1958). Argues for the case that actors' reasons can be seen as causes of their actions; see DAVIDSON (1963); WHITE (1968).

MALTHUS, T. R. (1798). *An Essay on the Principle of Populations.* In two convenient editions: (i) Ann Arbor: University of Michigan Press, 1959; (ii) London: Macmillan, 1966. (1803): *An Essay on the Principle of Population.* London: Dent, 1914. The original, polemical essay and the later, more considered thinking of the classic theorist of the relation between human populations and their resources. See DAVIS (1956); EVERSLEY (1959); FLEW (1957); U.N. (1953).

MATRAS, J. (1963–64). 'Religious observance and family formation in Israel: some inter-generational changes', *American Journal of Sociology* 69: 464–75. See BACHI, MATRAS (1962; 1964); MATRAS, AUERBACH (1962); TALMON-GARBER (1959).

MATRAS, J. (1965a). 'The social strategy of family formation: some variations in time and space', *Demography* 2: 349–62.

MATRAS, J. (1965b). 'Social strategies of family formation: some comparative data for Scandinavia, the British Isles and the United States', *International Social Science Journal* 17.

MATRAS, J. (1965–66). 'Social strategies of family formation: data for British female cohorts born 1831–1906', *Population Studies* 19: 167–81. See text (Ch. III). Matras develops and applies a technique for estimating the relative contribution of nuptiality and birth control to fertility. See also COALE (1967).

MATRAS, J., AUERBACH C. (1962). 'On rationalisation of family formation in Israel', *Milbank Memorial Fund Quarterly* 40: 453–80. See BACHI, MATRAS (1962; 1964) for work on same sample; also MATRAS (1963–64); TALMON-GARBER (1959).

MAULDIN, W. P. (1965a). 'Fertility studies: knowledge, attitude and practice' *Studies in Family Planning* (Population Council, New York) 7: 1–10. Compiles information on ideal family sizes in developing societies, but warns against its incomparability. See also BERELSON (1966); GLASS (1962); MAULDIN (1965b).

MAULDIN, W. P. (1965b). 'Application of survey techniques to fertility studies', *in* SHEPS, RIDLEY (1965): 93–118. Good study of sources and extent of low reliability and lack of validity in field surveys on fertility, containing examples of questions that have been administered in various studies on the same topic and the various results that they have elicited. Concludes that despite these difficulties surveys have an essential part to play in gathering information that censuses can never have. See MAULDIN (1965a).

MAULDIN, W. P. (1966). 'Estimating rates of population growth', *in* BERELSON (1966): 635–53. Because of the situation which registration is deficient in 60 per cent of Middle and South America, 90 per cent of Asia (excluding the

U.S.S.R.), and 95 per cent of Africa, techniques are necessary for estimating rates in these areas. Mauldin discusses some, including those that use the concept of the stable population. See COALE, ZELNIK (1963).

MAY, D. A., HEER, D. M. (1968). 'Son survivorship motivation and family size in India: a computer simulation', *Population Studies* 22: 199–210. If every mother were to practise fully effective birth control after son survivorship assured, reduction in intrinsic rate of increase would only be 24%; son survivorship not assured until wife is 32.6 years old. See LEIBENSTEIN (1957).

MAYER, A. C. (1960). *Caste and Kinship in Central India.* Berkeley and Los Angeles: University of California Press. An excellent field study that illuminates discussions in DRIVER (1963); BLAKE (1967b); NAG (1967); PAKRASI, MALAKER (1967). See also FOX (1967); COALE *et al.* (1965).

MAYER, K. B. (1952). *The Population of Switzerland.* New York: Columbia University Press.

MAZUR, D. P. (1967). 'Fertility among ethnic groups in the U.S.S.R.', *Demography* 4: 172–95. A study of 36 ethnic groups from the 1959 census; finds that four most crucial independent variables, in descending order, are the prevalence of traditional religion, the proportion of married women between 20 and 49, literacy and the male/female literacy differential. Does not discuss economic factors.

MAZUR, D. P. (1968). 'Birth control and regional differentials in the Soviet Union', *Population Studies* 22: 319–33. See text; and DAVTYAN (1967); SADVOKASOVA (1967); URLANIS (1967); HEER (1968a).

MCHUGH, P. (1968). *Defining the Situation: the Organisation of Meaning in Social Interaction.* Indianapolis: Bobbs-Merrill. Independent, critical inspection of nature, conditions for description of, and functions of norms/rules; see Ch. VI.

MCMILLAN, R. T. (1964). *Demographic and Socio-economic Correlates of Fertility in Trinidad and Tobago.* Washington: Agency for International Development, Office of International Training. See also BLAKE (1961); BRAITHWAITE, ROBERTS (1961); MORTARA (1961).

MEADE, J. E. (1968). *The Growing Economy.* London: Allen and Unwin, 'Population growth and the standard of living': pp. 147–87. A recent and sophisticated discussion of the inter-relations between demography and the economy. See also UNITED NATIONS (1967); OHLIN (1967).

MEHLAN, K.-H. (1966). 'The socialist countries of Europe', *in* BERELSON. (1966): 207–26. See also SZABADY *et al.* (1966) and references therein.

MEUVRET, J. (1965). 'Demographic crisis in France from the sixteenth to the eighteenth century', *in* GLASS, EVERSLEY (1965): 507–22. See text.

MICHEL, A. (1967). 'Interaction and family planning in the French urban family', *Demography* 4: 615–25. See text; and, for similar discussions, GOLDBERG (1958); HILL, STYCOS, BACK (1959); RAINWATER (1965). For other French material: 'ETUDE . . .' (1966); FEBVAY (1960); MICHEL (1967); PAILLAT (1962); PRESSAT (1967); SUTTER, BASTIDE (1963).

MINCER, J. (1963). 'Market prices, opportunity costs and income effects', *in* CHRIST, C. F. (ed.): *Measurement in Economics: Studies in Mathematical Economics and Econometrics in Memory of Yehuda Grunfeld.* Stanford: Stanford University Press: 67–82 ('Income and family size', pp. 75–79). See text. Makes BECKER's (1960) assumption that fertility varies directly with income when contraceptive efficiency is high; see BLAKE (1968); EASTERLIN (1969).

MIRO, C. A. (1966). 'Some misconceptions disproved: a programme of comparative fertility surveys in Latin America', *in* BERELSON (1966): 615–34. See text (Ch. III).

MIRO, C. A., RATH, F. (1965). 'Preliminary findings of comparative fertility surveys in three Latin American cities', *Milbank Memorial Fund Quarterly* 43: 36–68. Sample of c. 2,300 women, aged 20–50 in all marital statuses, taken between 1963 and 1964 in Panama City, Rio de Janeiro and San José by CELADE (L.A. Demographic Centre). See text (Ch. III).

MORSA, J. (1966). 'The Tunisia survey: a preliminary analysis', *in* BERELSON (1966): 581–93.

MORTARA, G. (1961). *Le Unioni Conjugali Libere nell'America Latina*. Roma: Istituto di Demografia, Universita di Roma. On consensual unions in Latin America. See also BLAKE (1961); BRAITHWAITE, ROBERTS (1961); STYPOS (1964); HILL, STYPOS, BACK (1959).

MORTARA, G. (1964). *Characteristics of the Demographic Structure of the American Countries*. Washington: Inter-American Statistical Institute, Pan-American Union. See also COLLVER (1965).

MURAMATSU, M. (1960). 'Effect of induced abortion on the reduction of births in Japan', *Milbank Memorial Fund Quarterly* 38: 152–66.

MURAMATSU, M. (1966). 'Japan', *in* BERELSON (1966): 7–19.

MURAMATSU, M., HARPER, P. A. (eds.) (1966). *Population Dynamics.* Baltimore: Johns Hopkins. A collection of sixteen somewhat general conference papers on family planning in developing countries. See also BERELSON (1966); BEHRMAN (1969); KISER (1962); SHEPS, RIDLEY (1965); BOGUE (1967).

MYRDAL, A. (1941). *Nation and Family*. New York: Harper; reprinted with an introduction by MOYNIHAN, D. P., Cambridge: M. I. T. Press, 1968. 'The Swedish experiment in democratic family and population policy'. Classic study, arising out of concern by Alva and Gunnar Myrdal about Sweden's imminently declining population in 1930s; arguing that a population policy should, first, be rooted in a general family policy and, second, pay particular attention to values. First-class exercise in applied sociology; also source of much information on Sweden before the War. Moynihan argues, in introduction, that argument here is relevant to U.S.A. today.

NAG, M. *Factors affecting human fertility in non-industrial societies: a cross-cultural study*. New Haven: Yale University Department of Anthropology. A compilation, similar to but more exhaustive than Ford's (1945; 1952), of data from the Yale Cross-Cultural Area Files on the intermediate variables affecting fertility in non-literate societies. Nag finds 61 societies in which one or more of these variables has a reportedly marked negative effect on fertility; nevertheless, there is no way of assessing the exact demographic significance of such variables. See text (Ch. III). And also LORIMER (1954); FORD (1945; 1952); DEVEREUX (1955); FIRTH et al. (1936; 1959; 1957).

NAG, M. (1967). 'Family type and fertility', *in* UNITED NATIONS DEPARTMENT OF ECONOMIC AND SOCIAL AFFAIRS: *World Population Conference* 1965, II, New York: United Nations: 160–63. Casts doubt on the frequently asserted connection between joint-family structure and high fertility (LORIMER, 1954; DAVIS, 1955). See also DRIVER (1963); MAYER (1960); PAKRASI, MALAKER (1967); BLAKE (1967b).

NATIONAL INSTITUTE OF CHILD HEALTH AND DEVELOPMENT. The Reproduction Information Centre at the National Institute (Bethesda Maryland 20014) is to publish an abstract journal on family planning and related areas (including the demographic). For further details, inquire to the Institute.

NELSON, W. O. (1965). 'Current research on new contraceptive methods', *in* SHEPS, RIDLEY (1965): 481–86. See also LAURENCE (1966); TIETZE (1965b).

OHLIN, P. G. (1961). 'Mortality, marriage and growth in pre-industrial populations', *Population Studies* 14: 190–97. A summary of his unpublished Ph.D. thesis (Harvard): 'The positive and preventive check: a study of the rate of growth of pre-industrial population'. Analyses the role of changing marriage patterns in fertility trends. See HAJNAL (1965).

OHLIN, G. (1967). *Population Control and Economic Development*. Paris: Development Centre of the Organisation for Economic Co-operation and Development. An excellently lucid and brief examination of the relationship between population growth and economic development, with special reference to the developing countries. Argues that there is no necessary relationship between the two variables, and contains a good discussion of the concepts of 'optimum population. and 'optimum rate of population growth'. See LEIBENSTEIN (1957); MEADE (1968)

PAILLAT, P. (1962). 'Influence du nombre d'enfants sur le niveau de vie de la famille: évolution de 1950 à 1961', *Population* 17: 421–42. Discovers relative deterioration of the living standard of 2+—child families as against 1—child

ones in France in the period. See also 'ÉTUDE . . .' (1966); FEBVAY (1960);
MICHEL (1967); PRESSAT (1967); SUTTER, BASTIDE (1963).

PAKRASI, K., MALAKER, C. (1967). 'The relationship between family type and
fertility', *Milbank Memorial Fund Quarterly* 45: 451–60. 1,018 couples from 3
major socio-economic groups. See NAG (1967); BLAKE (1967b); MAYER (1960);
DRIVER (1963); and text.

PAN, C. L. (1966). 'An estimate of the long-term crude birth rate of the agricultural
population of China', *Demography* 3: 204–08. See also TAUBER, ORLEANS
(1966); TIEN (1964–65). Hints at explanation of fertility of rural Chinese population are contained in MOORE, B.: *Social Origins of Democracy and Dictatorship.*
London: Allen Lane, 1967.

PEARL, R. (1939). *The Natural History of Population.* London: Oxford University
Press. The final summary of Pearl's famous inter-war arguments that populations grow logistically. Pearl's point that differential human fertility is a function of differential contraceptive use and effectiveness, and the measures that
he derived for the latter, have been challenged by several workers; see especially
POTTER (1966; 1967).

PEARL, R. (1940). 'Pregnancy rates and coitus rates', *Human Biology* 12 545–58.
See above.

PEEL, J., POTTS, M. (1969). *Textbook of Contraceptive Practice.* Cambridge: Cambridge
University Press. Useful compendium and explanatory accounts.

PETERSEN, W. (1960). 'The demographic transition in the Netherlands', *American
Sociological Review* 25: 334–47; reprinted in his *The Politics of Population.* Garden
City N.Y.: Doubleday, 1965: 166–92. A classic study. See, for a similar general
caution against too simple an interpretation of the transition thesis, DBVIS (1963).

PETERSEN, W. (1961). *Population,* New York: Macmillan. A standard, sociologically
informed introduction.

POHLMAN, E. (1965). 'Wanted and unwanted: towards less ambiguous definition',
Eugenics Quarterly 12: 19–27. A psychologist's discussion of a crucial issue if
utility models are going to be practical for those individuals whose preferences
are not clearly expressed. Pohlman has extended his work in a book not seen at
the time of writing: *The Psychology of Birth Planning.* Cambridge: Schenkman,
1968.

POTTER, J. (1965). 'The growth of population in America, 1700–1860', *in* GLASS,
D. V., EVERSLEY, D. E. C. (eds.): *Population in History.* London: Arnold: 631–79.
See also COALE, ZELNIK (1963); YASUBA (1962). Probably over-estimates incidence
and effect of mortality.

POTTER, R. G. (1961). 'Length of the fertile period', *Milbank Memorial Fund Quarterly*
39: 132–62.

POTTER, R. G. (1963–64). 'Birth intervals: structure and change', *Population Studies*
17: 155–66. A breakdown of the concept of birth interval into its components:
pregnancy, pregnancy wastage, post-partum amenorrhoea, anovulatory cycles
and time required for conception after ovulation is established. An examination
of the two types of birth interval for which data are available: that characteristic
of young Western mothers who do not nurse their babies and resume sexual
relations relatively soon after parturition; and those (mostly non-Western) who
nurse their babies and postpone the resumption of sexual relations for a longer
time.

POTTER, R. G. (1966). 'Application of life-table techniques to contraceptive effectiveness', *Demography* 3: 297–304; substantially reprinted in UNITED NATIONS DEPART-
MENT OF ECONOMIC AND SOCIAL AFFAIRS: *World Populations Conference* 1965, II,
New York: United Nations, 1967: 301–04. An important methodological
article; see PEARL (1939).

POTTER, R. G., NEW, M. L., WYON, J. B., GORDON, J. E. (1965). 'A fertility differential
in eleven Punjabi villages', *Milbank Memorial Fund Quarterly* 43: 185–201. 95%
of all wives, 15–44, with husbands present; 90% of those over 45: N = 2232.
India–Harvard–Ludhiana Population Study. Comparison of Jats (farmers)
and Chamar (leather workers).

POTTER, R. G., SAGI, P. C., WESTOFF, C. F. (1962). 'Knowledge of the ovulatory cycle and coital frequency as factors affecting conception and contraception', *Milbank Memorial Fund Quarterly* 40: 46–58. A revised version of this article appears *as* Chapters III and V of WESTOFF, C. F., POTTER, R. G., SAGI, P. C.: *The Third Child: a Study in the Prediction of Fertility*. Princeton: Princeton University Press, 1963: 26–37, 45–55. Finds, at first sight surprisingly, that 'couples who strive to speed pregnancy take longer . . . than those who report no special efforts'. This appears to be due, first, to ignorance of the timing and length of the fertile period and, second, to the fact that couples who make such attempts are often the subfecund ones. See POTTER, WESTOFF, SAGI (1963).

POTTER, R. G., WESTOFF, C. F., SAGI, P. C. (1963). 'Delays in conception: a discrepancy re-examined', *Eugenics Quarterly* 10. Empirical estimate of the likelihood of conception in the first interval, suggesting lower values than had been assumed to hold. See JAMES (1963–64; 1964–65).

PRESSAT, R. (1962). 'The ideal and the actual number of children', *Demográfia* 5: 415–26. National probabilities of reaching the ideal family size.

PRESSAT, R. (1967a). 'Opinions sur la fécondité et mesure de la fécondité', *Population* 22: 239–54. A critical discussion of the usefulness of the notion of 'ideal family size'. See PRESSAT (1962); GLASS (1962).

PRESSAT, R. (1967b). 'Les aléas de la natalité francaise', *Population* 22: 611–28. Documents the shift, familiar in other industrial societies in the West, away from childlessness, families of 1 and 4+ and into 2–3. See also BLAYO (1968); 'ETUDE . . .' (1966); FEBVAY (1960); MICHEL (1967); PAILLAT (1962); PRESSAT (1967a) (1969); SUTTER, BASTIDE (1963).

PRESSAT, R. (1969). 'Les naissances en France de 1964 à 1980', *Population* 24: 417–26. Birth-cohort of 1931; see PRESSAT (1967b).

RAINWATER, L., WEINSTEIN, K. K. (1960). *And the Poor get Children*. Chicago: Quadrangle. A penetrating study of the marital relations of 95 lower-class white couples in Chicago and Cincinatti and the extent to which they affect contraceptive practice. See also RAINWATER (1965).

RAINWATER, L. (1965). *Family Design: Marital Sexuality, Family size and Contraception*. Chicago: Aldine. See also RAINWATER (1960). Sociologically perhaps the most informative of all field studies on fertility: see discussion in IV. A study of 152 couples and 50 men and 55 women not married to each other in Chicago, Cincinnati and Oklahoma City. Analytically most similar to HILL, STYCOS, BACK (1959).

RAZZELL, P. (1965). 'Population change in eighteenth-century England: a reinterpretation', *Economic History Review* 2nd ser. 18: 312–32.

RAZZELL, P. (1967). 'Population Growth and Economic Change in eighteenth- and early nineteenth-century England', *in* JONES, E. L., MINGAY, G. (eds.): *Land, Labour and Population*. London: Arnold: 260–281. Statement, first, of contentious thesis that population growth in eighteenth-century England largely due to mortality control through smallpox innoculation, and, second, of why such control did not lead to famine that struck Ireland. See also KRAUSE (1967); CONNELL (1950); DAVIS (1963).

REINHARD, M., ARMENGAUD, A. (1968). *Histoire Générale de la Population Mondiale*. Paris: Editions Montchrestien. A very good general summary, deficient only in its misleading discussion of the causes of changes in the age-structure of populations. 3rd edition.

RELE, J. R. (1963). 'Fertility differentials in India: evidence from a rural backbackground', *Milbank Memorial Fund Quarterly* 41. 183–99. 2380 couples in central rural areas of Banaras Tehsil, Uttar Pradesh, 1956. Inverse relation between caste and fertility; no relation between caste and surviving children. Also finds support for HEER (1966); see MAY, HEER (1968).

RELE, J. R. (1965). 'Trends and differentials in the American age at marriage', *Milbank Memorial Fund Quarterly* 43: 219–34. See also POALE, ZELNIK (1963); YASUBA (1962)

RIDLEY, J. C. (1959). 'Number of children expected in relation to non-familial activities of the wife', *Milbank Memorial Fund Quarterly* 37: 277–96. See text;

and WHELPTON, CAMPBELL, PATTERSON (1966); UNITED NATIONS (1953); FREEDMAN, BAUMERT, BOLTE (1958–59); STYCOS, WELLER (1968); FEDERICI (1968).

RIZK, H. (1963). 'Social and psychological factors affecting fertility in the United Arab Republic', *Marriage and Family Living* 25: 69–73. 1960 Egyptian census data. See also ABU-LUGHOD (1963–64; 1965); YAUKEY (1961).

ROBERTS, G. W. (1968). 'The present fertility position in Jamaica', *in* SZABADY, E. (ed.): *World Views of Population Problems*. Budapest: Akadámiai Kaidó: 259–75. Differentials by educational attainment and type of union. See BLAKE (1961); BRAITHWAITE, ROBERTS (1961); MORTARA (1961); STYCOS (1964).

ROBERTS, G. W., CUMMINS, G. T., BYRNE, J., ALLEYNE, C. (1967). 'Knowledge and use of birth control in Barbados', *Demography* 4: 576–600. Good knowledge in visiting unions; good use in both these and marriages; males largely responsible for introduction of techniques; attainment of 'functional literacy', i.e. 4+ years schooling necessary for knowledge and use. See ROBERTS (1968) and other references there.

ROBINSON, W. C. (1963). 'Urbanisation and fertility: the non-western experience', *Milbank Memorial Fund Quarterly* 41: 291–308. Survey of reported urban-rural fertility ratios in many developing countries in 1950s. Argues that as fertility often measured by child-woman ratio, infant mortality often uncontrolled; when controlled, various ratios appear. Also discusses different meaning that urbanisation has in various countries. See text (Ch. V).

ROGERS, E. (1961). *The Diffusion of Innovations*. New York: Free Press. A standard study, applying the 'theory' to the diffusion of new farming techniques in the Middle West. See also COLEMAN, KATZ, MENDEL (1957); CARLSSON (1966–67).

ROMERO, H. (1966). 'Chile', *in* BERELSON (1966): 235–47. See also COLLVER (1965); MORTARA (1964); MIRO (1966); STYCOS (1962).

ROUSSEAU, J. J. (1755). *Discours sur l'Origine et les Fondements de l'Inégalité parmi les Hommes*. A convenient edition is: *The Social Contract and Discourses*. London: Dent, Everyman, 1914, reprinted.

ROWNTREE, G., PIERCE, R. M. (1961–62). 'Birth control in Britain', *Population Studies* 15: 3–31, 121–60. A national probability sample (drawn from an area south of the Caledonian Canal) of 3,000 men and women, 16–69, taken in 1959–60. The standard source for Britain, together with Lewis–Faning (1949). The Population Investigation Committee, London School of Economics is carrying on this work at present (1969): see text. See also GREBENIK, ROWNTREE (1963); HENRY (1962).

RUSSELL, J. C. (1948). *British medieval population*. Albuquerque: University of New Mexico Press. English poll tax records of 1377, together with more fragmentary sources. Argues for a relatively late age at marriage. See, for similar thesis, HOMANS (1942); for counter-argument, HAJNAL (1965).

RUSSETT, B. M. *et al.* (1964). *World Hand-book of Social and Political Indicators*. New Haven: Yale University Press: 373–75. Section on fertility. See FRIEDLANDER, SILVER (1967).

RYDER, N. B. (1956). 'La mesure des variations de la fécondité au cours du temps', *Population* 11: 29–46. A full discussion of the relative usefulness of period and cohort measures, with reference to the fertility rates recorded for Western countries after the Second World War. See UNITED NATIONS (1957); RYDER (1969).

RYDER, N. B. (1959). 'Fertility', *in* HAUSER, DUNCAN: 400–36. Excellent review of the nature of the data and the problems they present; contains more socio-logical speculation than the otherwise similar 1965 article.

RYDER, N. B. (1963–64). 'Notes on the concept of a population', *American Journal of Sociology* 69: 447–63. A thorough review of the nature of the basic population model and discussion of its applications to some problems of common concern to demographers and sociologists. 'The concept of a population is advocated as a frame of reference in investigations of population composition and process, in the resolution of differences between macroanalysis and microanalysis, and in the design of studies of social change'. Probably the best single introduction to the demographic *perspective* for sociologists. See also STINCHCOME (1968).

RYDER, N. B. (1964). 'The process of demographic translation', *Demography* 1: 74–82. The method for translating period rates into more informative cohort ones.

RYDER, N. B. (1965). 'The measurement of fertility patterns', *in* SHEPS, RIDLEY, (1965): 287–306. The clearest single account of measures of fertility. See also RYDER (1959).

RYDER, N. B. (1969). 'The emergence of a modern fertility pattern: United States, 1917–66', *in* BEHRMAN. The most sophisticated attempt yet made on any demographic data to disentangle the relative contribution of changes in the total quantity of nuptiality and fertility and changes in the timing of those events to observed cohort fertility rates. In particular, Ryder is able to attach relatively precise weights to the contribution of the trends away from one child and four or more, to the fall in the mean age of marriage and in the mean age of fertility.

RYDER, N. B., WESTOFF, C. F. (1967). 'Oral contraception and American birth rates', *in* LIU, W. (ed.): *Family and Fertility*. Notre Dame and London: University of Notre Dame Press: 171–83. The first evaluation of the demographic effect of the pill in the United States. Ryder and Westoff conclude that there may be a relation between fertility decline and increasing use of the pill, but admit that a causal link cannot yet be established with certainty: what, for example, would the relevant couples have been doing if the pill had not been available? See WESTOFF, RYDER (1967) for an assessment of the incidence of use of the pill in the United States in 1965.

RYDER, N. B., WESTOFF, C. F. (1967). 'The trend of expected parity in the United States, 1955, 1960, 1965', *Population Index* 33: 153–67. An assessment of the predictions made from the 1955 and 1960 GAF data (FREEDMAN, WHELPTON, CAMPBELL, 1959; WHELPTON, CAMPBELL, PATTERSON, 1966). Concludes that the GAF studies over-estimated the decline in cohort fertility, as a result of not foreseeing a rise in the age of childbearing and making inter-, rather than merely intra-cohort, standardisations. Recommends more scepticism about the usefulness of expectations as predictors.

SADVOKASOVA, E. A. (1967). 'Birth control measures and their influence on population replacement', *in* UNITED NATIONS DEPARTMENT OF ECONOMIC AND SOCIAL AFFAIRS: *World Population Conference* 1965, II, New York: United Nations: 110–14. SUMMARY OF SOVIET DATA. See also DAVTYAN (1967); URLANIS (1967); MAZUR (1967); HEER (1968a).

SAMUEL, T. J. (1965). 'Social factors affecting fertility in India', *Eugenics Review* 57: 5–15. Few clear occupational differentials (cf. DRIVER (1963); POTTER *et al.* (1965)); literacy only effective with wives of high school education; no relation with joint-family structure (see NAG (1967); PAKRASI, MALAKER (1967)).

SAUVY, A. (1952; 1954). *Théorie Générale de la Population*, I: *Économie et Population*, II: *Biologie Sociale*. Paris: Presses Universitaires de France. Already a classic, by France's leading demographer and first director of the I.N.E.D. At present being translated into English.

SAUVY, A. (1958). *Fertility and Survival: population problems from Malthus to Mao Tse-tung*. New York: Criterion, 1961. Originally published in French as *De Malthus à Mao Tse-tung: le problème de la population dans le monde*, Paris: Denoël.

SCHNEIDER, E. B., KRUPP, S. (1964–65). 'An illustration of the use of analytical theory in sociology: the application of the economic theory of choice to non-economic variables', *American Journal of Sociology* 70: 695–703.

SCHNEIDER, J. R. L. (1963). 'Fertility changes during and after the Second World War in England and Wales and Sweden', Ph.D. London University. See GLASS (1968).

SCHWARTZ, K. (1965). 'Nombre d'enfants suivant le milieu physique et social en Allemagne', *Population* 20: 77–92. Thoroughly reviews a range of factors, including income: best analysed data for the FDR. See FREEDMAN, BAUMERT, BOLTE (1958–59).

SEKLANI, M. (1960). 'La fécondité dans les pays arabes', *Population* 5: 831–56. See also KIRK (1967); and RIZK (1963); YAUKEY (1961).

SHAPIRO, S., JONES, E. W., DENSEN, P. M. (1962). 'A life table of pregnancy termination and correlates of foetal loss', *Milbank Memorial Fund Quarterly* 40: 7–45, Data from 6,844 pregnancies in the New York area in 1958 and 1959 which. together with those from FRENCH, BIERMAN (1962), are used in calculations of fecundability and natural fertility.

SHEPS, M. C. (1965). 'Applications of probability models to the study of patterns of human reproduction', *in* SHEPS, RIPLEY (1965): 307–32.

SHEPS, M. C. (1965–66). 'An analysis of reproductive patterns in an American isolate', *Population Studies* 19: 65–80. A demographic analysis of data gathered on 736 marriages among the Hutterites in 1958–61 (and 73 observed in 1953). See EATON, MAYER (1953); TIETZE (1957); and JAMES (1963–4; 1964–5). SHEPS, working with PERRIN and RIDLEY, is developing probability models for predicting fertility rates under certain sets of conditions. These have not been discussed here, but reference can be found to them in this paper and in more recent issues of the American and British journals. See also BODMER, JACQUARD (1969).

SHEPS, M. C., PERRIN, E. B. (1963). 'Some changes in birth rates as a function of contraceptive effectiveness: some applications of a stochastic model', *American Journal of Public Health* 53: 1031–46. See also POTTER (1966; 1967); and SHEPS (1965).

SHEPS, M. C., RIDLEY, J. C. (eds.) (1965). *Public Health and Population Change: current research issues.* Pittsburgh: University of Pittsburgh Press, A first-class collection of 27 authoritative papers covering all aspects of population studies, organised in the conviction that these studies are essentially inter-disciplinary. Unfortunately weakest on the social determinants of fertility, but not to be ignored for that.

SIEBERT, S., SUTTER, J. (1963). 'Attitudes devant la maternité: une enquête à Grenoble', *Population* 18: 655–82. An important modern French source; see also 'LA LIMITATION . . .' (1956); WEILL-HALLÉ (1967); BERGUES *et al* (1960).

SILVER, M. (1965). 'Births, marriages and business cycles in the United States', *Journal of Political Economy*: 237–55.

SILVER, M. (1965–66). 'Births, marriages and income fluctuations in the United Kingdom and Japan', *Economic Development and Cultural Change* 14: 302–15. See text. U.S. 1871–1961; Japan 1878–1938, 1951–57; U.K. 1870–1958. See also GALBRAITH, THOMAS (1941); KIRK, NORTMAN (1958); KIRK (1960); TELLA (1960).

SIMON, H. (1957). *Models of man.* New York: Wiley. A discussion of the usefulness and implications of models postulating utility maximisation. See also SIMON (1966).

SIMON, H. (1966). 'Theories of decision-making in economics and behavioural science', *in* AMERICAN ECONOMIC ASSOCIATION, ROYAL ECONOMIC SOCIETY: *Surveys of Economic Theory, III: Resource Allocation.* London: Macmillan, New York: St. Martin's Press: 1–28. An excellent review and critical discussion, together with bibliography, of the modifications that have had to be and will have to be made to the simple behavioural assumptions of classical economics if those assumptions are to accurately reflect and thus more precisely predict reality. Of especial interest to the argument in Chs. IV and VI are the sections on the notion of utility-maximisation, on the relevance of actors' expectation-formations and on the problems raised by discrepancies between the objective choices open to an actor and the choices as he perceives them. Simon (1957) elsewhere discusses in detail his concept of 'satisficing'.

SINHA, R. P. (1962). 'Urbanisation and fertility differentials', *Journal of Social Research* 5: 63–68. See ROBINSON (1963).

SMITH, T. E. (1960–1). 'The Cocos-Keeling Islands: a demographic laboratory', *Population Studies* 14: 94–130. Together with the Hutterites, the modern population with the highest gross reproduction rate. See COALE (1965); EATON, MAYER (1953); TIETZE (1957); SHEPS (1965–6).

SPENGLER, J. J. (1966). 'Values and fertility analysis', *Demography* 3: 109–30. Examination of analytic usefulness of 'value' and 'goal'; see text Ch. VI.

SPENGLER, J. J., DUNCAN, O. D. (eds.) (1956). *Population Theory and Policy,* Glencoe: Free Press. A somewhat dated but still useful introduction.

SPIRO, M. E. (1968). 'Virgin birth, parthenogenesis and physiological paternity:

an essay in cultural interpretation', *Man* n.s. 3: 242–61. See LEACH (1966); correspondence in *Man* n.s. 3 (1968); 4 (1969) *passim*.

SRB, V., KUČERA, M., VYUŠILOVA, D. (1964). 'Une enquête sur la prévention des naissances et le plan familial on Tséchoslovaquie', *Population* 19: 79–94. See also SZABADY *et al.* (1966) and references therein; KLINGER (1966); MEHLAN (1966).

STEVENSON, R. F. (1968). *Population and Political Systems in Tropical Africa*. New York: Columbia University Press. Refutation of Evans-Pritchard/Fortes hypothesis of no relation between density and political systems: higher density, more state-like. Ibo an exception. Careful about imputing causality. See also LOCKRIDGE (1968).

STEWART, C. M. (1962–3). 'Family allowance statistics in Great Britain', *Population Studies* 16: 210–18. From these figures can be inferred the closer child-spacing in marriage.

STINCHCOMBE, A. L. (1968). *Constructing Social Theories*. New York. Harcourt. An excellent introduction, containing a simple account of demographic explanation. See RYDER (1963–4).

STOETZEL, J. (1955). 'Les attitudes et la conjoncture démographique: la dimension idéale de la famille', *Proceedings of the World Population Conference* 1954, VI, New York: United Nations, 1019–33. See text; and GLASS (1962).

STOTT, D. H. (1962). 'Cultural and natural checks on population growth', *in* ASHLEY MONTAGU (ed.): *Culture and the Evolution of Man*. New York: Oxford University Press: 355–76. An examination of the evidence on the demographic effects of various social pressures in animals and of the extent to which such processes occur in human societies. Stott concludes that they do, and documents them. Considerable scepticism is expressed by physiologists, but no formal refutation has been published at the time of writing. See JAMES (1969).

STONE, L. (1961). 'Marriage among the English nobility in the sixteenth- and seventeenth-centuries', *Comparative Studies in Society and History* 3: 182–215. See also HOLLINGSWORTH (1957; 1964); HENRY, LEVY (1960); HAJNAL (1965).

STYCOS, J. M. (1962). 'A critique of the traditional planned parenthood approach in underdeveloped areas', *in* KISER, C. V. (ed.): *Research in Family Planning*. Princeton: Princeton University Press. See also DAVIS (1967); BANKS, BANKS (1964).

STYCOS, J. M. (1962–63). 'Culture and differential fertility in Peru', *Population Studies* 16: 257–70. See text; and HEER (1964–65); HEER and TURNER (1964–65); JAMES (1966–67); HEER (1967); WHITEHEAD (1968); BRADSHAW (1969).

STYCOS, J. M. (1964). *The Control of Human Fertility in Jamaica*. Ithaca: Cornell University Press. See also BLAKE (1961).

STYCOS, J. M. (1965). 'Needed research on Latin American fertility: urbanisation and fertility', *Milbank Memorial Fund Quarterly* 43: 299–323; also *in* his *Human Fertility in Latin America: Sociological Perspectives*. Ithaca: Cornell University Press, 1968: 270–88. Surveys research to date. The 1968 volume contains 18 of Stycos' many articles on L. A. fertility and the problems it raises.

STYCOS, J. M. (1968). 'Education and fertility in Latin America', *in* his *Human Fertility in Latin America: Sociological Perspectives*. Ithaca: Cornell University Press: 250–69.

STYCOS, J. M., WELLER, R. H. (1967). 'Female working roles and fertility', *Demography* 4: 210–17. See text.

STYS, W. (1957–58). 'The influence of economic conditions on the fertility of peasant women', *Population Studies* 11: 136–48. See text (Ch. V). HAWLEY (1955).

SUTTER, J., BASTIDE, H. (1963). 'The causes of the increase in the birth rate in France', *Revue du Practicien* (Paris) 13 (June 21): 2207–15. See BLAYO (1968); 'ETUDE . . .' (1966); FEBVAY (1960); MICHEL (1967); PAILLAT (1962); PRESSAT (1967); 2, GLASS (1968).

SUTTON, G. F., WUNDERLICH, G. S. (1967). 'Estimating marital fertility rates by educational attainment using a survey of new mothers', *Demography* 4: 135–42. Probability sample of 3,726 mothers having children in 1963. Highest fertility in those with 1–3 yrs. high school and 1+ yrs. college; college women have same curve of family building over time but start 5 yrs. later on average. See text; and WESTOFF, POTVIN (1966); HUBBACK (1955).

SZABADY, E. (ed.) (1964). *Fertility and Social Mobility*. Budapest: Akadémiai Kaidó. Papers on the relations between mobility (and other socio-economic factors) and fertility in Eastern Europe. See also BERENT (1951–52); BLAU, DUNCAN (1967); DUNCAN (1966).

SZABADY, E. (1968). 'Basic fertility tables for some East-European socialist countries', *in* his (ed.): *World Views of Population Problems*. Budapest: Akadémiai Kaidó: 387–408. See SZABADY *et al.* (1966).

SZABADY, E., TEKSE, K., PRESSAT, R. (1966). 'La population des pays socialistes européens: la fécondité', *Population* 21: 941–70. Contains extensive bibliography. See also SZABADY (1968).

TABAH, L., VIET, J. (1966). *Démographie: Tendances Actuelles et Organisation de la Recherche. 1955–65*. Paris, The Hague: Mouton. The first part contains an annoted bibliography of demographic work and related studies published between 1955 and 1965, and the rest of the book a description of work in progress, research and teaching centres, etc. See also KISER (1968); LEGEARD (1966).

TAKESHITA, J. Y. (1966). 'Lessons learned from family planning studies in Taiwan and Korea', *in* BERELSON, (1966): 691–710. See also TAKESHITA (1967); BERELSON, FREEDMAN (1954); TAUBER (1961); FREEDMAN, PEN, TAKESHITA, SUN (1963); FREEDMAN, TAKESHITA, SUN (1964); FREEDMAN (1965); COLLVER, SPEARE, LIU (1966–67).

TAKESHITA, J. Y. (1967). 'Birth control in some of the developing countries of the Far East', *in* UNITED NATIONS DEPARTMENT OF ECONOMIC AND SOCIAL AFFAIRS: *World Population Conference* 1965, II, New York: United Nations: 168–71.

TALMON-GARBER, Y. (1959). 'Social structure and family size', *Human Relations* 12: 121–46. Relates perceptions of family structure in *kibbutzim* to fertility intentions: see GOLDBERG (1958); RAINWATER (1965); and for other Israeli data BACHI, MATRAS (1962; 1964); MATRAS (1963–64); MATRAS, AUERBACH (1962).

TAUBER, I. (1958). *The Population of Japan*. Princeton: Princeton University Press. An authoritative study. See also MURAMATSU (1960; 1966); DAVIS (1963).

TAUBER, I. (1961). 'Population growth in a Chinese microcosm: Taiwan', *Population Index* 27: 101–26. See also FREEDMAN, PEN, TAKESHITA, SUN (1963); FREEDMAN, TAKESHITA, SUN (1964); FREEDMAN (1964); COLLVER, SPEARE, LIU (1966–67); TAUBER, ORLEANS (1966).

TAUBER, I., ORLEANS, L.A. (1966). 'Mainland China', *in* BERELSON (1966): 31–54. See also TIEN (1964–65). The Office of Population Research at Princeton University is at present undertaking a thorough demographic study of the Chinese Peoples' Republic.

TELLA, A. (1960). 'The economic cycle in marriages', *National Industrial Conference Board Business Record* 17: 20–22, 25. See text; and GALBRAITH, THOMAS (1941); KIRK, NORTMAN (1958); KIRK (1960); SILVER (1965; 1965–66).

TIEN, H. Y. (1964–65). 'Sterilisation, oral contraception and population control in China', *Population Studies* 18: 215–36. See also TAUBER, ORLEANS (1966).

TIETZE, C. (1957). 'Reproductive span and rate of reproduction among Hutterite women', *Fertility and Sterility* 8: 89–97. See EATON, MAYER (1953); SHEPS (1965–66); JAMES (1963–64; 1964–65).

TIETZE, C. (1964). 'The demographic significance of legal abortion in Eastern Europe', *Demography* 1: 119–25. A good source from an authority on fertility control. See SZABADY *et al.* (1966).

TIETZE, C. (1965a). 'Induced abortion and sterilisation as methods of fertility control', *in* SHEPS, RIDLEY (1965): 400–16. A good summary.

TIETZE, C. (NATIONAL COMMITTEE ON MATERNAL HEALTH INC.) (1965b). *Bibliography on Fertility Control* 1960–65, New York: National Committee on Maternal Health. 1,935 references on all aspects of fertility control. The N.C.M.H. has since become part of the Population Council Inc. (Bio-Medical Division), 2 East 103rd Street, N.Y. 10029. This division is publishing a revised and updated bibliography on fertility control.

TIETZE, C., POTTER, R. G. (1963). 'A statistical model of the rhythm method', *in*

MILBANK MEMORIAL FUND: *Emerging Techniques in Population Research*. New York: Milbank Memorial Fund; 141–58.

TOUTAIN, J. C. (1963). *La Population de France de* 1700 *à* 1959, Paris: Institute de Science Économique Appliquée.

'UNE ENQUÊTE sur la prévention des naissances et le plan familial en Hongrie,' (1965). *Population* 20: 126–30. See GOOD (1964); SZABADY *et al.* (1966); SZABADY (ed.) (1964). (1962).

UNITED NATIONS DEPARTMENT OF ECONOMIC AND SOCIAL AFFAIRS (1953). *The Determinants and Consequences of Population Trends*. New York: U.N. ST/SOA/Series A/17; 53. XIII. 3. An excellently documented summary of all important speculation and research to 1952. See EVERSLEY (1959).

UNITED NATIONS DEPARTMENT OF ECONOMIC AND SOCIAL AFFAIRS (1954). *Foetal, Infant and Early Childhood Mortality*, I, *The Statistics*, II, *Biological, Social and Economic Factors*. New York: United Nations, ST/SOA/Series A/13 and Add. 1; 54. IV. 7 and 54. IV. 8. An old but still informative source on abortion rates.

UNITED NATIONS DEPARTMENT OF ECONOMIC AND SOCIAL AFFAIRS (1956). *The Ageing of Populations and its Economic and Social Implications*. New York: United Nations. ST/SOA/Series A/26; 56. XIII. 6. A standard examination of the relative contribution of changes in fertility and mortality rates to the ageing of populations.

UNITED NATIONS DEPARTMENT OF ECONOMIC AND SOCIAL AFFAIRS (1957). *Recent Trends of Fertility in Industrialised Countries*. New York: United Nations. ST/SOA/ Series A/27; 57. XIII. 2. A now somewhat dated comparative analysis of the recovery in the birth rate in various countries during and after World War II. For later material, see UNITED NATIONS (1965); RYDER (1956; 1969).

UNITED NATIONS DEPARTMENT OF ECONOMIC AND SOCIAL AFFAIRS (1962). *The Mysore Population Study*. New York: United Nations. A detailed and important study of an area of high fertility in India.

UNITED NATIONS DEPARTMENT OF ECONOMIC AND SOCIAL AFFAIRS (1965a): 'Conditions and trends of fertility in the world', *Population Bulletin of the United Nations* (no. 7, 1963), New York: United Nations. ST/SOA/Series N/7; 64. XIII. 2. An examination of fertility rates, with special reference to the non-industrialised countries, together with information on rural-urban and socio-economic differentials. See UNITED NATIONS (1957; 1965b).

UNITED NATIONS DEPARTMENT OF ECONOMIC AND SOCIAL AFFAIRS (1965b). *Demographic Yearbook*. 1965, New York: United Nations. The standard secondary source of world population statistics, published annually one year after the year in question. The 1965 volume is devoted mainly to natality statistics, the latest to be so. See UNITED NATIONS (1957; 1965a).

UNITED NATIONS DEPARTMENT OF ECONOMIC AND SOCIAL AFFAIRS. 'Population and vital statistics report', *Statistical Papers*, Series A. A quarterly publication, usually between one and two years behind, of the latest statistics on total populations by country, together with birth, death and infant mortality figures and rates.

UNITED NATIONS DEPARTMENT OF ECONOMIC AND SOCIAL AFFAIRS (1967). *World Population Conference* 1965, IV, New York: United Nations. This volume contains papers of the relationships between demographic and economic factors; see also OHLIN (1967); MEADE (1968).

UNITED NATIONS LATIN AMERICAN DEMOGRAPHIC CENTRE (CELADE) (1965). 'Rural fertility in Chile: results of a pre-test', *Demography* 2: 97–114.

URLANIS, B. T. (1967). 'Dynamics of the birth rate in the U.S.S.R. and factors contributing to it', *in* UNITED NATIONS DEPARTMENT OF ECONOMIC AND SOCIAL AFFAIRS: *World Population Conference* 1965, II, New York: United Nations: 232–38. Attributes much of the low fertility to female employment: see the criticism in MAZUR (1968); also DAVTYAN (1967); SADVOKASOVA (1967); MAZUR (1967); HEER (1968a).

U.S. BUREAU OF THE CENSUS (1961–). *U.S. Census of Population* 1960. Washington: Government Printing Office. The most recent decennial census. Full details n KISER, GRABILL, CAMPBELL (1968); BOGUE (1969). Reports PC(2)-3A (Women by number of children ever born), PC(2)–3B (Childspacing), PC(2)–3C (Women by number of children under 5 years old) of especial interest.

VALAORAS, V. G., POLYCHRONOPOULOU, A., TRICHOPOULOS, D. (1964–65). 'Control of family size in Greece: the results of a field survey', *Population Studies* 18: 265–78.

VAN DE WALLE, E. (1968). 'Marriage and marital fertility', *Proceedings of the American Academy of Arts and Sciences* 97: 486–501. A study of France, Switzerland, Belgium and the Netherlands, estimating the relative contribution of changes in the age at marriage and birth control to the fertility transition in these countries. See text; and COALE (1967); MATRAS (1965a; 1965b) 1965–66); DEMENY (1968a).

VAN HEEK, F. (1956–57). 'Roman Catholicism and fertility in the Netherlands: demographic aspects of minority status', *Population Studies* 10: 125–38. See DAY (1968); PETERSEN (1960); BURCH (1966); and text (Ch. V).

VAVRA, Z.: 'Taux de natalité en ville et à la campagne', *Demografia* 4 (1962): 529–36. Hungary.

VIELROSE, E. (1968). 'Family budgets and birth rates', *in* SZABADY, E. (ed.): *World Views of Population. Problems.* Budapest: Akadémiai Kaidó: 359–63. Family budgets of Polish workers in 1963. Calculates extent of competition between consumption of babies and consumer goods, esp. cars. Predicts that the competition will gradually cease.

VINCENT, P. (1961). *Recherches sur la Fécondité Biologique.* Paris: Presses Universitaires de France. Still a standard source on calculations and estimations of natural fertility rates. Vincent's data is unique in being taken from a population which is neither historical, nor from a primitive or developing society, nor from a modern isolate. Instead he analysed the fertility of the couples with nine or more children in France after 1918 during a national scheme to increase fertility.

VOGT, J. (1964). 'Component parts of the number of births', *Statsφnomisk Tidsskrift* (Oslo) 78: 287–307.

WEILL-HALLE, L. (1967). *La Contraception et les Français.* Paris: Maloine. Follow-up survey on use of contraceptives (including I.U.D.s and oral contraceptives) and abortion of 7,600 couples who had attended clinics of the French Family Planning Movement, 1956–66. Despite return of only 2,947 usable completed questionnaires, the authors consider their results reasonably valid for married, but not for unmarried, respondents. See BERGUES *et al.* (1960); 'La limitation . . .' (1965).

WEINTRAUB, R. (1962). 'The birth rate and economic development: an empirical study', *Econometrica* 40: 812–17. The partial regression and correlation coefficients of the 1953–54 crude birth rates on mean per capita income, proportion of farm population and mean infant mortality rate for 30 developed and underdeveloped nations. See text; and ADELMAN (1963); ADELMAN, MORRIS (1965–66); HEER (1966); FRIEDLANDER, MORRIS (1967).

WESTOFF, C. F. *et al.* (1954). 'The use, effectiveness and acceptability of various methods of fertility control', *in* WHELPTON, KISER (1954): IV, 885–951.

WESTOFF, C. F., POTTER, R. G., SAGI, P. C. (1961–62). 'Some estimates of the reliability of survey data on family planning', *Population Studies* 15: 52–69. Useful article, arising from experience on the Princeton study: see WESTOFF, POTTER, SAGI, MISHLER (1961); WESTOFF, POTTER, SAGI (1963).

WESTOFF, C. F., POTTER, R. G., SAGI, P. C., MISHLER, E. G. (1961). *Family Growth in Metropolitan America.* Princeton: Princeton University Press. In Westoff, *et al.* (1963), below, the authors summarise this, the first of the so-called 'Princeton Studies', as follows: 'In the first few months of 1957 we interviewed a sample of 1,165 women all of whom had given birth to their second child about six months earlier'. (The sample was restricted to white women only, registered in one of the eight largest Standard Metropolitan Areas of the United States, excluding Boston, and who had been married once only, had been born in the United States, and who were still living with their husbands and had no expectancy of parting from him within six months). 'One of the questions we asked concerned the number of children they wanted to have. We also collected information on contraceptive practice, desired spacing of children, length of birth intervals, and on a wide variety of background information, attitudes and

11

behaviour. A basic interest then was to learn the kinds of factors relevant to the number of children American couples want to have. Accordingly, it was possible to analyse a wide array of social and psychological factors in relation to desired family size, birth intervals and fertility-planning success. The interrelations of spacing attitudes, desired family size, birth intervals, and contraceptive practice were also explored in greater detail than had been possible in previous studies'.

WESTOFF, C. F., POTTER, R. G., SAGI, P. C. (1963). *The Third Child: a Study in the Prediction of Fertility*. Princeton: Princeton University Press. See Westoff *et al*. (1961). 'In early 1960, three years later, we interviewed the same women again'. (In fact only 905 of the original 1,165). 'Three and a half years had now elapsed since their second child was born. Again we completed a lengthy interview with the woman, collecting data on her fertility over the three-year period as well as on changes in the social and economic status of the couple. This longitudinal feature of our study design also permitted us to include questions reflecting new leads gained from the analysis of the first interviews. The primary objective of this second phase of the study was to explain why some couples stopped at two children while others went on to have a third and even a fourth child during this interval of time. Thus the analysis of data collected in the second round of interviews was focused on trying to account for fertility since the second birth'. The Princeton Study is an essential source on almost all aspects of the social determinants of fertility.

WESTOFF, C. F., POTVIN, R. H. (1966). *College women and Fertility Values*, Princeton: Princeton University Press. Sample of 1st and 4th year students in a sample of 4-year colleges in U.S. Finds that college has little influence on number of children women wish to have (except in case of Catholic women in Catholic colleges). See HUBBACK (1955); SUTTON, WUNDERLICH (1967); KISER, FRANK (1967).

WESTOFF, C. F., RYDER, N. B. (1967). 'Methods of fertility control in the United States: 1955, 1960, and 1965', *in* LIU, W. T. (ed.): *Family and Fertility*. Notre Dame and London: University of Notre Dame Press: 157–69. See text. First evaluation of the incidence of use of the oral contraceptive pill in the United States. RYDER, WESTOFF (1967) evaluates its effect on fertility.

WHELPTON, P. K. (1954). *Cohort Fertility: Native White Women in the United States*. Princeton: Princeton University Press. The classic first application of the cohort approach to American fertility data. See GLASS, GREBENIK (1954); FREEDMAN, WHELPTON, CAMPBELL (1959); WHELPTON, CAMPBELL, PATTERSON (1966).

WHELPTON, P. K., CAMPBELL, A. A., PATTERSON, J. E. (1966). *Fertility and Family Planning in the United States*. Princeton: Princeton University Press. The second report of the Growth of American Families project. A similar sample to that obtained for the first study was interviewed to assess the distribution and explanations of the accuracy and otherwise of the fertility expectations expressed by the 1955 sample. The interviews were done in 1960. They differed from the first in covering non-whites for the first time, and from the Princeton Study in being nation-wide, and not restricted to one type of area. Since 1966, scepticism has been expressed about the reliability of fertility expectations for predictive purposes; see RYDER, WESTOFF (1967). First GAF study is FREEDMAN, WHELPTON, CAMPBELL (1959).

WHELPTON, P. K., KISER, C. V. (eds.) (1964; 1950; 1952; 1954; 1958). *Social and Psychological Factors Affecting Fertility*. New York: Milbank Memorial Fund. A sample of native white Protestant couples in Indianapolis, married between 1927 and 1929 when the wife was under 30, who had lived in the city for most of their lives and completed the eighth grade of high school. The first of the three extensive and intensive American field studies (the others being the Princeton Study, directly in line from this, and the GAF study).

WHITE, A. R. (ed.) (1968). *The Philosophy of Action*. London: Oxford University Press. Useful collection of articles with concise summary of issues by White. Contains DAVIDSON (1963); see also MACINTYRE (1967); WINCH (1958); GRUNER (1966).

WHITEHEAD, L. (1968). 'Altitude, fertility and mortality in Andean countries',

Population Studies 22: 335–46. See text; and STYCOS (1962–63); HEER (1964–65); HEER, TURNER (1964–65); JAMES (1966–67); DONAYRE (1966); HEER (1967); BRADSHAW (1969).

WINCH, P. (1958). *The Idea of a Social Science*. London: Routledge and Kegan Paul. Argues that to understand a human action is an activity different in kind from, and necessarily an alternative to, providing a causal explanation of it; and that talk of causality is therefore misplaced. See MACINTYRE (1967); DAVIDSON (1963); WHITE (1968).

WOLFERS, D. (1968). 'Determinants of birth intervals and their means', *Population Studies* 22: 253–62. WOLFERS argues that there are two sources of variability in birth intervals in a population: first, random variation around a mean value determined by the two probabilities, that of resumption of fecundity postpartum and of fecundability; and second, variation between different women in respect of these two values. JAMES' method is only appropriate in a population whose variatibility in this respect is of the former kind, and an alternative method must be devised for the latter. Such a method yields lower fecundabilty values on an observed population of women. See JAMES (1963–64; 1964–65).

WRIGLEY, E. A. (1966a). 'Family limitation in pre-industrial England', *Economic History Review* 2nd ser. 18: 82–109. A reconstruction of the births and fertility rates for Colyton, east Devon, between 1538 and 1837 (with special reference to the period between 1560 and 1790). A convincing demonstration of the existence of severe birth control by deliberate means in a pre-industrial population, and thus a caution to simple assumptions about such populations. Comparisons are made with Crulai (see GAUTIER and HENRY, 1958). See also WRIGLEY (1966b; 1969).

WRIGLEY, E. A. (ed.)(1966b). *An Introduction to English Historical Demography*. London: Weidenfeld and Nicolson. A description of the techniques adapted from French to English conditions by Cambridge Group for the History of Population and Social Structure. For an example of results, see WRIGLEY (1966a). EVERSLEY enters a plea for the more traditional methods of reconstruction.

WRIGLEY, E. A. (1968). 'Mortality in pre-industrial England: the example of Colyton, Devon, over three centuries', *Proceedings of the American Academy of Arts and Sciences* 97: 546–80. See WRIGLEY (1966a).

WRIGLEY, E. A. (1969). *Population and History*. London: Weidenfeld and Nicholson. A first-class, careful synthesis of much recent historical work; very illuminating on inter-relations between population and economy. Published too late to be used in text above. GLASS, EVERSLEY (1965).

WRONG, P. H. (1958a). 'Class fertility differentials before 1850', *Social Research* 25: 70–86.

WRONG, D. H. (1958b). 'Trends in class fertility in Western nations', *Candian Journal of Economics and Political Science* 24: 216–229. See also GLASS (1968); JOHNSON (1960); KISER (1960); WRONG (1960).

WRONG, D. H. (1960). 'Class fertility differentials in England and Wales', *Milbank Memorial Fund Quarterly* 38: 37–47. See also references above.

WRONG, D. (1961). *Population and Society*. New York: Random House. Simple but not naive introduction to the field from sociological standpoint.

WYATT, F. (1967). 'Clinical notes on the motives of reproduction', *Journal of Social Issues* 23: 29–56. Argues that motive lies in female's attempt to resolve problem of 'inner duality'. Freudian.

WYNNE-EDWARDS, V. C. (1962). *Animal Dispersion in Relation to Social Behaviour*. Edinburgh: Oliver and Boyd. Restatement of the hitherto rather discredited view that populations are homeostatically regulated around an optimum level. Illustrated with a wealth of evidence from non-human, and especially bird, populations. Subject of great dispute among animal ecologists. See CARR-SAUNDERS (1922); applications in WRIGLEY (1966a; 1969); DOUGLAS (1966).

YAUKEY, D. (1961). *Fertility Differences in a Modernising Country*. Princeton: Princeton University Press. Sample of 909 female Lebanese nationals (613 from Beirut; 296 from two nearby but isolated villages), married more than 5 years, of all statuses and both Christian and Muslim faith. Most useful source for Middle Eastern information. See also ABU-LUGHOD (1963–64; 1965); RIZK (1963).

ZARATE, A. O. (1967a). 'Some factors associated with urban-rural fertility differentials in Mexico', *Population Studies* 21: 283–93.

ZARATE, A. O. (1967b). 'Fertility in urban areas of Mexico: implications for the theory of demographic transition', *Demography* 4: 363–73. Analysis appears to confirm HEER (1966).

ZIKRY, A. M. (1964). 'Urbanisation and its effect on the levels of fertility of U.A.R. women', *L'Égypte Contemporaine* 55: 27–42. See also: ABU-LUGHOD (1963–64; 1965); RIZK (1963).

Subject Index

Entries do not include those sections indicated in the Contents: e.g. under 'Abortion' no entry will be found for pp. 47–50 and 95–6.